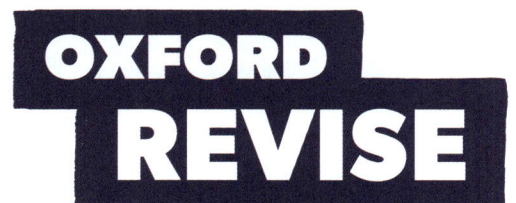

AQA GCSE

AN INSPECTOR CALLS

English Literature

COMPLETE REVISION AND PRACTICE

Series Editor: Lyndsay Bawden

Annie Fox

Contents

 Shade in each level of the circle as you feel more confident and ready for your exam.

| How to use this book | iv |

Plot 2–19

1 Act one 2
- Knowledge
- Retrieval

2 Act two 8
- Knowledge
- Retrieval

3 Act three 14
- Knowledge
- Retrieval

Methods 20–27

4 Writer's methods 20
- Knowledge
- Retrieval

Characters 28–63

5 Arthur Birling 28
- Knowledge
- Retrieval

6 Sybil Birling 34
- Knowledge
- Retrieval

7 Sheila Birling 40
- Knowledge
- Retrieval

8 Eric Birling 46
- Knowledge
- Retrieval

9 Gerald Croft 52
- Knowledge
- Retrieval

10 Inspector Goole 58
- Knowledge
- Retrieval

Themes 64–93

11 Social class and Inequality 64
- Knowledge
- Retrieval

12 Family and relationships	69
⚙ Knowledge	⊖
⇄ Retrieval	⊖

13 Money	74
⚙ Knowledge	⊖
⇄ Retrieval	⊖

14 Responsibility and guilt	79
⚙ Knowledge	⊖
⇄ Retrieval	⊖

15 Gender roles	84
⚙ Knowledge	⊖
⇄ Retrieval	⊖

16 Generations	89
⚙ Knowledge	⊖
⇄ Retrieval	⊖

Exam Skills and Sample Answers	94–102
⚙ Knowledge	⊖
⇄ Retrieval	⊖

Exam Practice	103–115
✎ Practice	⊖

How to use this book

This book uses a three-step approach to revision: **Knowledge**, **Retrieval**, and **Practice**. It is important that you do all three; they work together to make your revision effective.

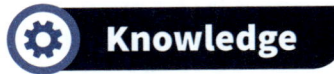

Knowledge

Knowledge comes first. Each chapter is divided into **Knowledge Organisers**. These are clear, easy-to-understand, concise summaries of the content that you need to know for your exam. The information is organised to show how one idea flows into the next so you can learn how everything is tied together.

Sample answers and examiner's comments are also provided where appropriate to help you understand what makes a good answer.

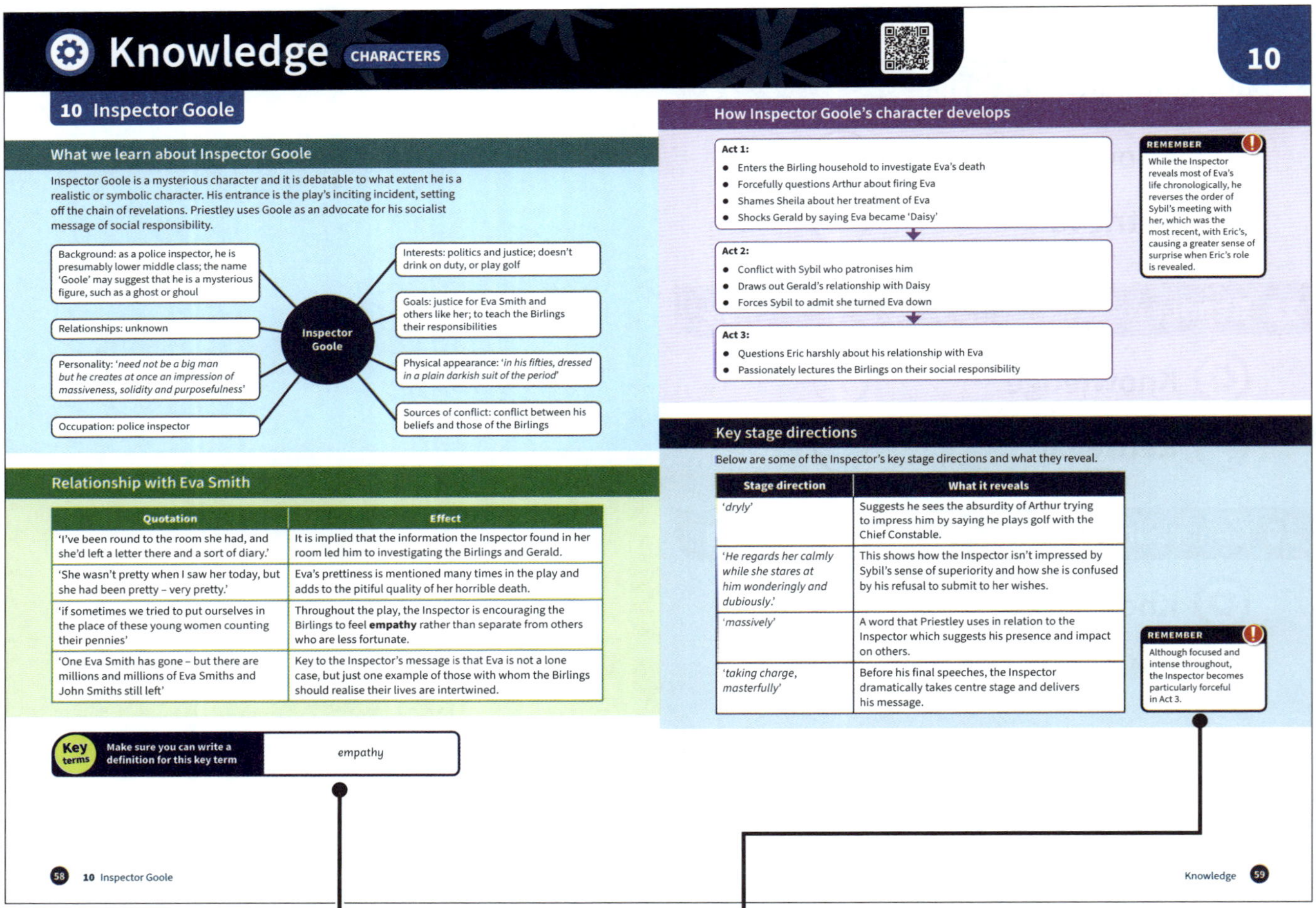

Knowledge CHARACTERS

10

10 Inspector Goole

What we learn about Inspector Goole

Inspector Goole is a mysterious character and it is debatable to what extent he is a realistic or symbolic character. His entrance is the play's inciting incident, setting off the chain of revelations. Priestley uses Goole as an advocate for his socialist message of social responsibility.

Inspector Goole
- Background: as a police inspector, he is presumably lower middle class; the name 'Goole' may suggest that he is a mysterious figure, such as a ghost or ghoul
- Relationships: unknown
- Personality: *'need not be a big man but he creates at once an impression of massiveness, solidity and purposefulness'*
- Occupation: police inspector
- Interests: politics and justice; doesn't drink on duty, or play golf
- Goals: justice for Eva Smith and others like her; to teach the Birlings their responsibilities
- Physical appearance: *'in his fifties, dressed in a plain darkish suit of the period'*
- Sources of conflict: conflict between his beliefs and those of the Birlings

Relationship with Eva Smith

Quotation	Effect
'I've been round to the room she had, and she'd left a letter there and a sort of diary.'	It is implied that the information the Inspector found in her room led him to investigating the Birlings and Gerald.
'She wasn't pretty when I saw her today, but she had been pretty – very pretty.'	Eva's prettiness is mentioned many times in the play and adds to the pitiful quality of her horrible death.
'if sometimes we tried to put ourselves in the place of these young women counting their pennies'	Throughout the play, the Inspector is encouraging the Birlings to feel **empathy** rather than separate from others who are less fortunate.
'One Eva Smith has gone – but there are millions and millions of Eva Smiths and John Smiths still left'	Key to the Inspector's message is that Eva is not a lone case, but just one example of those with whom the Birlings should realise their lives are intertwined.

Key terms Make sure you can write a definition for this key term: *empathy*

How Inspector Goole's character develops

Act 1:
- Enters the Birling household to investigate Eva's death
- Forcefully questions Arthur about firing Eva
- Shames Sheila about her treatment of Eva
- Shocks Gerald by saying Eva became 'Daisy'

Act 2:
- Conflict with Sybil who patronises him
- Draws out Gerald's relationship with Daisy
- Forces Sybil to admit she turned Eva down

Act 3:
- Questions Eric harshly about his relationship with Eva
- Passionately lectures the Birlings on their social responsibility

REMEMBER: While the Inspector reveals most of Eva's life chronologically, he reverses the order of Sybil's meeting with her, which was the most recent, with Eric's, causing a greater sense of surprise when Eric's role is revealed.

Key stage directions

Below are some of the Inspector's key stage directions and what they reveal.

Stage direction	What it reveals
'dryly'	Suggests he sees the absurdity of Arthur trying to impress him by saying he plays golf with the Chief Constable.
'He regards her calmly while she stares at him wonderingly and dubiously.'	This shows how the Inspector isn't impressed by Sybil's sense of superiority and how she is confused by his refusal to submit to her wishes.
'massively'	A word that Priestley uses in relation to the Inspector which suggests his presence and impact on others.
'taking charge, masterfully'	Before his final speeches, the Inspector dramatically takes centre stage and delivers his message.

REMEMBER: Although focused and intense throughout, the Inspector becomes particularly forceful in Act 3.

58 10 Inspector Goole

Knowledge 59

Key terms **Make sure you can write a definition for these key terms**

The **Key terms** box highlights the key words and phrases you need to know, remember, and be able to use confidently.

REMEMBER

The Remember box offers useful guidance.

LINK

The Link box offers a reference to a related topic.

REVISION TIP

Revision tips offer you helpful advice and guidance to aid your revision and help you to understand key concepts and remember them.

Retrieval

The **Retrieval questions** help you learn and quickly recall the information you've acquired. These are short questions and answers about the Knowledge Organiser content you have just revised. Cover up the answers with some paper and write down as many answers as you can from memory. Check back to the Knowledge Organisers for any you got wrong, then cover the answers and attempt all the questions again until you can answer *all* the questions correctly.

Make sure you revisit the Retrieval questions on different days to help them stick in your memory. You need to write down the answers each time, or say them out loud, for your revision to be effective.

Previous questions

Many Retrieval pages also have some **Retrieval questions** from **previous topics**. Answer these to see if you can remember the content from the earlier sections. If you get the answers wrong, go back and do the Retrieval questions for the earlier topics again.

Practice questions linked to the content you have just been revising are flagged here.

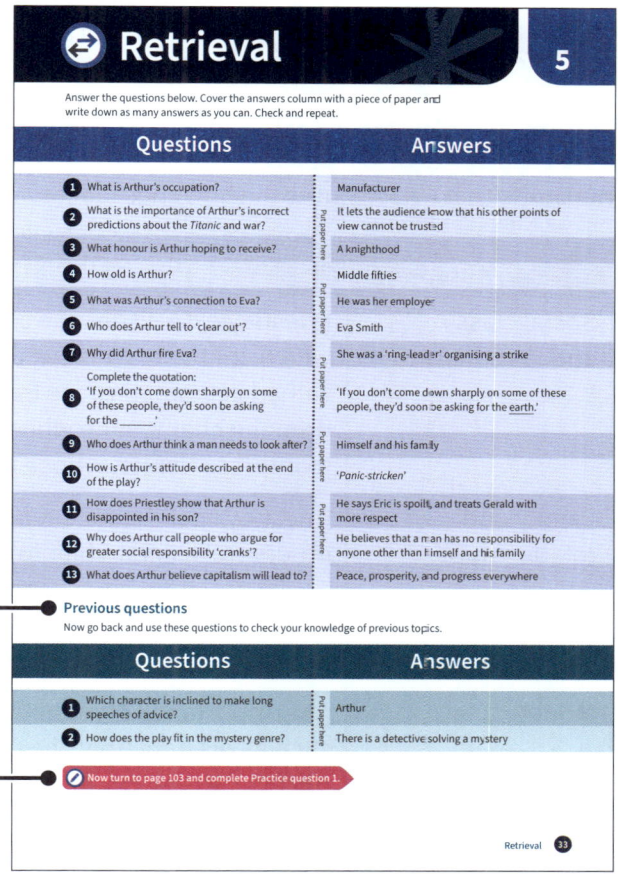

Practice

Once you are confident with the Knowledge Organisers and Retrieval questions, you can move on to the final stage: **Practice**. This can be found at the back of the book.

The **exam-style questions** in this section help you apply all the knowledge you have learned.

EXAM TIP

Exam tips show you how to interpret the questions, provide guidance on how to answer them, and give advice on how to secure as many marks as possible. Guidance is also offered on how to approach different command words.

Answers and Glossary

You can scan the QR codes at any time to access sample answers and mark schemes for the exam-style questions, a glossary containing definitions of the key terms, as well as further revision support, or go to go.oup.com/OR/GCSE/A/EngLit/Inspector

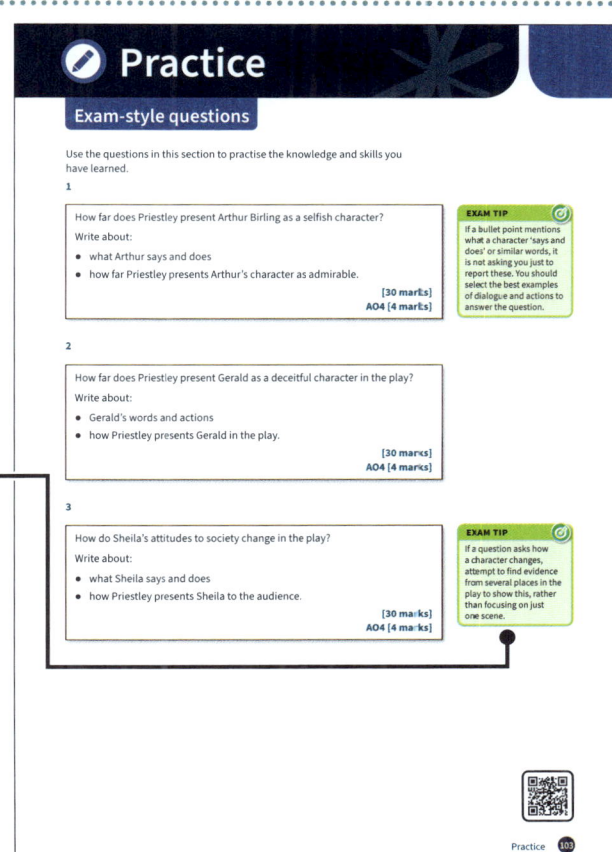

Knowledge — PLOT

1 Act one

Key ideas in Act one

Writing about the big ideas of the text is the most important aspect of your studies. But you also need to understand how these ideas are presented – the **methods** that Priestly uses to show these ideas.

Key idea	How this is presented and developed in Act 1
Social class and inequality	Priestley establishes the comfort and abundance of luxury available to the Birlings, which contrasts with Eva living in poverty. Arthur, as her employer, and Sheila, as a valued customer, cause Eva to become unemployed. It is ironic that the Birlings are drinking champagne while Eva has killed herself by drinking disinfectant. Arthur tries to impress Gerald, whose family has a higher social standing.
Family and relationships	Priestley uses Arthur's tendency to dominate the dialogue and his expectation that others will listen to him to support his portrayal of patriarchy and capitalism. Eric and Sheila are more equal, as shown in their teasing relationship. Although Sheila and Gerald have a warm, playful relationship, Priestley hints at some previous distance between them as part of his exploration of love.
Money	The importance of money to the Birlings is shown by Arthur's **explicit** references, such as his hope that the Crofts will work with the Birlings for 'lower costs and higher prices'. He fires Eva because she wanted the girls to receive a rise from 'twenty-two and sixpence' to 'twenty-five shillings' a week. It is a source of conflict that both Eric and the Inspector think he should have paid it.
Responsibility and guilt	Priestley uses Arthur and Sheila's contrasting **attitudes** towards their roles in Eva's life to highlight the theme of responsibility. Sheila immediately feels guilty, while Arthur views his actions as a sensible business decision.
Gender roles	Priestley presents the Birlings as an affluent family of the time, with Arthur at the head of the table and leading the conversation. At key moments, the women are expected to leave the room so the men can speak. Sheila's engagement to a socially impressive man like Gerald is considered a great success for the family.
Generations	Arthur takes great pleasure in lecturing the younger generation, who he thinks can learn from his hard-won experience. In contrast to Arthur's speech-making, Sheila and Eric speak more informally. After the announcement of Eva's death, Priestley shows the differences between the younger Birlings, who react emotionally, and Arthur, who is irritated but denies any involvement.

Key events of Act one

- The events of *An Inspector Calls* take place in 1912, two years before the outbreak of the First World War.
- The play begins after dinner with the Birling family seated in their dining room with their guest, Gerald Croft.
- Arthur Birling, the father of the family, is a prosperous manufacturer and they are celebrating his daughter Sheila's engagement to Gerald.

- Arthur makes a toast to his daughter, Sheila.
- Gerald presents an engagement ring to Sheila.
- Arthur tells the young people not to be pessimistic about the future, as capitalism will ensure they are protected.
- Arthur expresses excitement about future progress and downplays concerns about troubles with the workforce and an impending war.

- While having an after-dinner drink with Gerald, Arthur suggests that he is likely to receive a knighthood soon, unless there is some scandal.
- Arthur lectures his son, Eric, and Gerald about a man's responsibility to look after his own business and family, without regard for others.

- Inspector Goole arrives and tells them that a young woman, Eva Smith, has swallowed disinfectant and died at the infirmary.
- After being shown her photograph, Arthur admits that she was an employee whom he fired because she led a strike action for higher wages.

- The Inspector tells Sheila that Eva's next job was at a shop called Milwards.
- Sheila is shocked to discover that Eva was the shopgirl who she was responsible for getting fired after becoming jealous of her.

- The Inspector reveals that Eva Smith changed her name to Daisy Renton, a name which Gerald clearly recognises.
- After the Inspector leaves the dining room, Sheila confronts Gerald, realising that he had a relationship with Daisy Renton.

- The Inspector reappears and looks at Sheila and Gerald 'searchingly'.

REVISION TIP
You will never be expected to simply recount the play's plot, but you should know the order of events well enough that you can quickly reference relevant sections of the play in your answer.

LINK
You can read more about capitalism on page 31 and in Themes on pages 74–78.

REMEMBER
Act 1 ends on a **cliffhanger**, with this revelation of Gerald's involvement with Eva. Noting structural devices like this is one way of analysing the writer's methods.

Knowledge

Knowledge — PLOT

1 Act one

The beginning of Act one

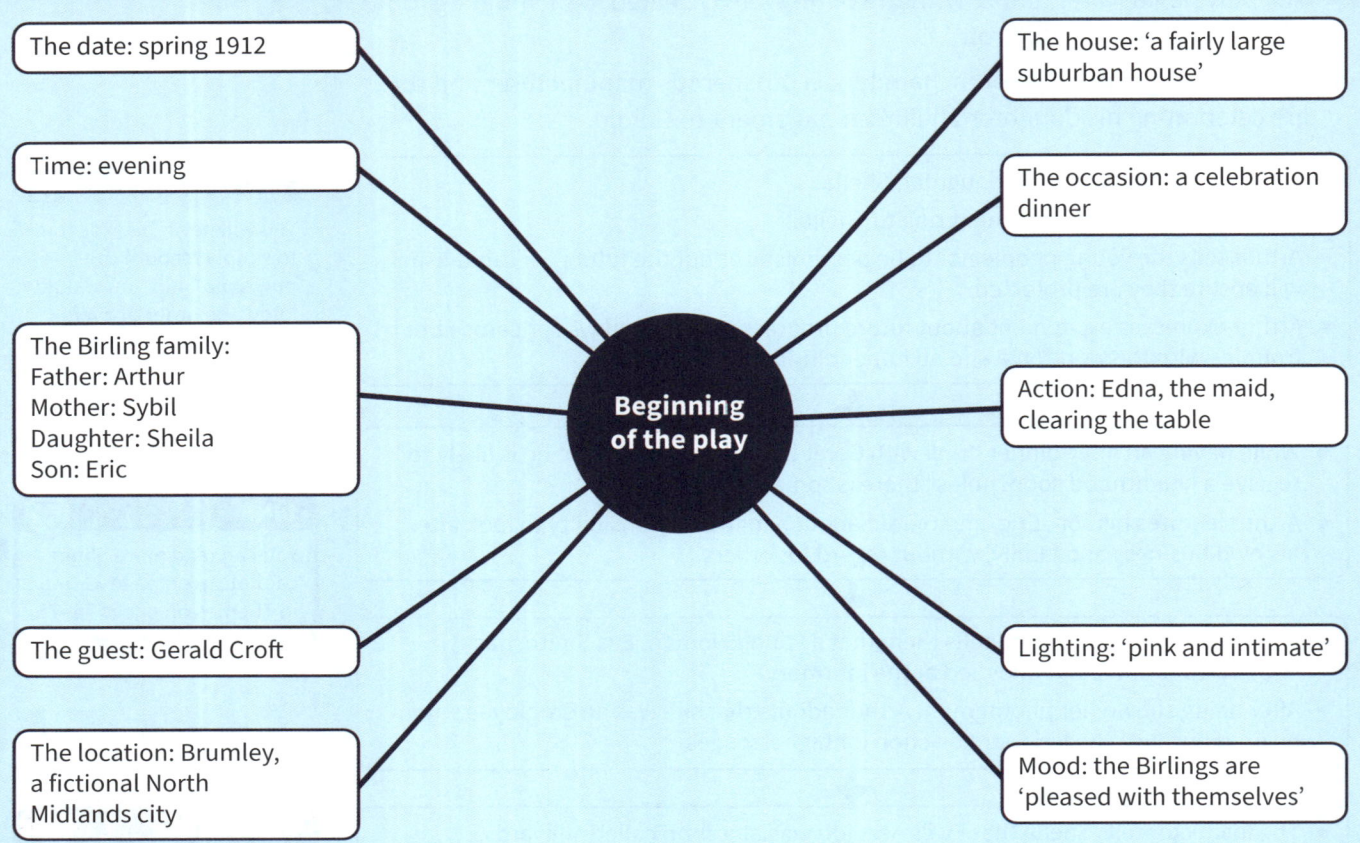

- The date: spring 1912
- Time: evening
- The Birling family:
  Father: Arthur
  Mother: Sybil
  Daughter: Sheila
  Son: Eric
- The guest: Gerald Croft
- The location: Brumley, a fictional North Midlands city
- The house: 'a fairly large suburban house'
- The occasion: a celebration dinner
- Action: Edna, the maid, clearing the table
- Lighting: 'pink and intimate'
- Mood: the Birlings are 'pleased with themselves'

Centre: Beginning of the play

REMEMBER
You will need to show that you have understood the context of the play relevant to the question, such as the characters' circumstances, social class, and beliefs. You need to explain the different methods that are used, such as stage directions, to answer the question.

REMEMBER
Although J.B. Priestley wrote *An Inspector Calls* in 1945, he set it in 1912, so that the characters in the play are unaware of events that occurred after 1912 (such as the First and Second World Wars), unlike the playwright and audience.

REVISION TIP
Revise the characters' names and relationships so that you don't confuse them in the exam.

REVISION TIP
The themes of social class and inequality are important in the play. Note how often money and social advantages are mentioned in the play, creating a contrast with Eva Smith's life.

What the audience learns in Act one

What we learn	Evidence	Effect on character/plot
The Birlings are a comfortable upper middle class family.	The house is that of a 'prosperous manufacturer'. Edna, the parlourmaid, is clearing the remnants of a luxurious meal: 'champagne', 'dessert plates'. The men are dressed in 'tails and white ties', that is, formal evening clothes. Most of the characters are drinking – Eric is 'squiffy' (drunk).	The initial setting establishes the comfort of the Birling family, as well as creating an aspect of formality to the gathering, which is a 'special occasion'. This abundance will later contrast with what we learn of Eva's poverty. Priestley shows the solidity and comfort of the family shattering as the play continues.
There are small suggestions of **tension** between Gerald and Sheila.	Sheila reminds Gerald of a time last summer when he 'never came near' her. She, 'half playful, half serious', warns him to 'be careful'.	This **foreshadows** the later revelation that Gerald had been in a relationship with Daisy Renton that summer.
Arthur Birling is entirely unaware of the sad events that are to occur.	Arthur declares this is 'one of the happiest nights of my life' and makes optimistic predictions about the future, such as avoiding war and the success of the *Titanic*, a ship which, later, tragically sank.	Arthur is portrayed through his long speeches and self-satisfied proclamations as being oblivious to the tragedies that will befall not only his own family, but also the world at large.
The entrance of the Inspector entirely changes the mood of the play.	He declines Arthur's attempts at hospitality and starkly declares that a girl has killed herself: 'Burnt her inside out, of course'.	The Inspector quickly takes control of the scene, despite Arthur's attempts to remain in charge. His shocking announcement contrasts with the celebratory family gathering.
The Inspector is determined to make the Birlings and Gerald accept their responsibility for Eva Smith's sad death.	He is pursuing 'one line of inquiry at a time' so that he can present the case for each character's guilt.	The gradual revelation of each character's responsibility for Eva's death and their different reactions propels the **plot**.

LINK
To learn more about the method of foreshadowing, see page 25.

 Key terms Make sure you can write a definition for these key terms

attitude   cliffhanger   explicit   foreshadowing
method   plot   tension   turning point

Knowledge

Knowledge — PLOT

1 Act one

Turning points in Act one

Key turning point	Key quotations	Effect
The family celebrates Sheila and Gerald's engagement.	• Sheila: 'You're squiffy!' • Arthur: 'It's one of the happiest nights of my life.' • Sheila: 'Now I really feel engaged.'	Priestley establishes a festive, celebratory mood, with Arthur's expansive speeches and generosity, as well as indicating the benefits of capitalism to this particular family.
Inspector Goole announces Eva Smith's death.	• Inspector: 'she'd swallowed a lot of strong disinfectant. Burnt her inside out, of course.' • Eric: 'My God!' • '*They are surprised and rather annoyed.*'	This **turning point** creates shock and confusion, as well as irritation for Arthur, who doesn't want the celebration interrupted. This is the catalyst for Priestley's exploration into responsibility and guilt.
Arthur Birling admits he fired Eva.	• Arthur: 'she'd had a lot to say – far too much – so she had to go.' • Eric: 'Well, I think it's a dam' shame.'	Arthur is defensive and uncomfortable at the revelation of his responsibility for Eva's death, but maintains it was a sound financial decision. This is an early example of the division between the generations, as Eric disagrees with his father and feels differently about his attitude to money.
Sheila realises she shares responsibility for Eva's downfall.	• Sheila: 'How could I know what would happen afterwards?' • Sheila: 'I'll never, never do it again to anybody.'	Sheila is also implicated in Eva's death, but her reaction **contrasts** with her father's as she is regretful and anguished. Priestley is exposing more differences in attitude between the family members.
Gerald confesses to Sheila that he had been with Daisy Renton/Eva Smith.	• Gerald: 'I'm sorry, Sheila. But it was all over and done with, last summer.'	Through the name change, Priestley introduces another twist: that Gerald was involved with the dead woman. This has implications for his relationship with Sheila. Priestley presents him as embarrassed and defensive at his own actions being revealed.
Sheila tells Gerald that the Inspector already knows.	• Sheila: 'Why – you fool – *he knows*. Of course he knows.'	In her bitter response, Sheila reveals her early understanding of the power of the Inspector, which Priestley presents as almost supernatural. This turning point is the climax of the first act.

REVISION TIP
Consider how Priestley uses each turning point to increase the dramatic tension and alter the relationships between the characters. For example, by the end of Act 1, the celebratory mood has entirely soured. Sheila now has regrets.

REMEMBER
When you are responding to a question you will need to show that you have understood the significance of relevant key events in the play, such as turning points.

Retrieval

Answer the questions below. Cover the answers column with a piece of paper and write down as many answers as you can. Check and repeat.

#	Questions	Answers
1	In what year is the play set?	1912
2	What method does Priestley use to hint at problems in Gerald and Sheila's relationship?	Foreshadowing
3	To whom is Sheila engaged?	Gerald
4	What is the importance of the comfortable setting of the Birlings' home in conveying important ideas in the play?	Their upper-class home contrasts with the poverty that Eva lived in, conveying Priestley's themes concerning social class and money
5	What prop does the Inspector show Arthur?	A photograph
6	Why did Arthur fire Eva?	She helped organise a strike
7	What was the last steady job Eva had?	Working at Milwards
8	Why does the Inspector think Sheila got Eva fired?	Sheila was jealous of Eva
9	What name did Eva begin using?	Daisy Renton
10	Who is accused of getting 'squiffy'?	Eric
11	Complete the quotation: 'It's one of the _____ nights of my life.'	'It's one of the <u>happiest</u> nights of my life.'
12	Complete the quotation: 'Burnt her _____ _____, of course.'	'Burnt her <u>inside</u> <u>out</u>, of course.'
13	Who does Sheila call 'a fool'?	Gerald
14	Complete the quotation: 'Why – _____ _____ – he knows.'	'Why – <u>you</u> <u>fool</u> – he knows.'
15	In Act 1, which character does Priestley present as dominating the dialogue, showing his comfort in his role in society?	Arthur
16	Why is the Inspector's entrance an important turning point in Act 1?	It changes the mood and introduces the tragedy of Eva Smith

Now turn to page 103 and complete Practice questions 1–3.

Knowledge — PLOT

2 Act two

Key ideas in Act two

Key ideas	How methods are used to show these ideas
Social class and inequality	Priestley shows Sybil's confident sense of class privilege in her dealings with the Inspector. The difference in social class between Eva and Gerald is emphasised by Sheila suggesting that Gerald must have seemed like a 'fairy prince' to Eva. Sybil notes that the father of Eva's baby 'didn't belong to her class'.
Family and relationships	Priestley's use of conflict, tension, and interruptions shows the increasing divisions in the family. Sheila returning her engagement ring to Gerald symbolises the break in their relationship. Sheila and Sybil are presented as opposites in their interactions with the Inspector.
Money	Throughout the play, Priestley's discussion of money is explicit, including specfic sums, to emphasise its importance in society. Eva's lack of money, so severe that she is hungry, is contrasted with Gerald's wealth. When they part, he gives her 'a gift of money'. The Brumley Women's Charity Organisation is another source of money, but Sybil chooses to withhold aid from Eva on flimsy grounds, leading to her death.
Responsibility and guilt	Social and personal responsibility are explored by Sybil's supposedly socially-aware activities with a charity, and the family's individual personal guilt. Priestley highlights through Sheila's emphatic dialogue how guilty she feels compared to others. Sybil, in particular, claims to be guilt-free. Only in the final moments of the act does she begin to realise her error.
Gender roles	Repeatedly, characters try to get Sheila to leave the room in order to shield her from unpleasantness. The Inspector replies: 'And you think young women ought to be protected against unpleasant and disturbing things?' This is ironic, since no one shielded Eva from much worse things. Priestley shows the limited opportunities available to a woman of Eva's class without a family to support her.
Generations	Priestley exposes the faults in this supposedly happy family and the generational divisions. The family treats Eric as if he is still 'a boy' and has little respect for him. Sheila is called an over-excited 'child'. However, Sheila is shown to be the quickest at grasping what the Inspector is doing and what is at stake for the family.

Key events of Act two

- Act 2 of An Inspector Calls begins as Act 1 finished, with the cliffhanger, after it is revealed that Gerald knew Eva when she was calling herself 'Daisy Renton'.
- The Inspector is in the doorway of the room observing Gerald and Sheila, whose intense exchange he has interrupted.

- Gerald asks the Inspector if Sheila can be excused, but Sheila wants to hear the Inspector's questioning of Gerald.
- Sybil asserts that the girl's death has nothing to do with them.
- The Inspector says again that Eva Smith 'became' Daisy Renton.
- Gerald confesses that he put Daisy up in a friend's flat, supporting her for months while they had a relationship.
- Sheila returns Gerald's ring to him.

- When the Inspector shows Sybil a photograph of Eva, she at first denies that she knows her.
- The Inspector says that Sybil, an influential member of a charity organisation, turned down Eva's appeal for assistance due to her perceived 'impertinence'.

- The Inspector reveals that Eva was pregnant.
- Sybil asserts that it is the father of the baby who is responsible for Eva.
- Sybil says she didn't believe Eva when she said she wouldn't take money from the father because he drunkenly admitted he had stolen it.
- Sybil says the baby's father should be forced to confess all.
- Despite Sheila's warning, Sybil realises too late that it is her son, Eric, who was the baby's father.

- Eric enters 'pale and distressed'.

REVISION TIP

The audience learns much more about Sybil in Act 2, where she is the focus of much of the Inspector's questioning, therefore Act 2 is a likely focus of a question about her character.

LINK

You can read more about props, stage directions, and cliffhangers in Methods on pages 21–23.

Knowledge — PLOT

2 Act two

Beginning of Act two

Beginning of Act 2

- Time: evening, immediately follows **climactic** end of Act 1

  This unbroken timeline starts the act with high tension.

- Action: the Inspector interrupts Gerald and Sheila's argument

- Emotions:
  - Sheila speaks to Gerald 'with hysterical laugh'
  - Gerald speaks to the Inspector 'with an effort'

  This highlights Gerald's attempt to remain controlled while Sheila's emotions are on the surface.

  Sheila's laugh symbolises her rejection of how Mrs Birling treated Eva Smith. Priestley presents Sheila's emotional response as necessary for change and reform.

- Dialogue:
  - brief questions from the Inspector
  - Gerald tries to persuade the Inspector and Sheila that Sheila should go.

- **Conflict:** Sheila and Gerald argue over whether or not she should stay.

  This reveals more about the relationship between these characters, and helps to **convey** Priestley's ideas about gender roles.

  Notice how often the word 'hysterical' is attributed to Sheila and her strong emotions.

  Priestley uses this to show characters attempting to attack Sheila personally rather than address the socialist message she's trying to convey.

- Mood: tense and unsettled

  This contrasts with the cheerful beginning of Act 1.

> **REVISION TIP**
> When considering how the characters develop, you might contrast Gerald and Sheila's relationship at the beginning of Act 1 with their conflict in Act 2.

> **REVISION TIP**
> Use mind maps or bullet points to note what you learn about each of the characters throughout the play.

> **LINK**
> You can read more about the use of structure, the handling of time, cliffhangers, and dialogue in Methods on pages 21–23.

> **REMEMBER**
> You will need to write about the methods that Priestley uses in the drama. For example, his stage directions and dialogue heighten the conflict and tense mood in the opening of Act 2.

What the audience learns in Act two

What we learn	Evidence	Effect on character/plot
Gerald and Sheila are no longer presented as a united couple.	Gerald accuses Sheila of only wanting 'to see somebody else put through it'. Sheila says: 'I must obviously be a selfish, vindictive creature.'	Priestley shows the changing nature of relationships through the sudden change in how Sheila and Gerald view each other, in contrast to the beginning of Act 1. She now doubts that he ever loved her.
Sybil does not grasp what has happened before her entrance and underestimates the Inspector.	Sybil thinks it's 'morbid curiosity' to continue the conversation. She tries to impress the Inspector with the family's importance: 'my husband was lord mayor'.	Priestley presents Sybil as unfeeling and superior, in contrast with Sheila's guilt and vulnerability, further developing the theme of differences between generations.
Sheila tells her mother how much Eric has been drinking, which Gerald confirms.	'He's been steadily drinking too much for the last two years.' 'I have gathered he does drink pretty hard.'	This follows hints about Eric's drinking in the first act and foreshadows how his heavy drinking influenced his relationship with Eva.
Under the Inspector's questioning, Gerald reveals the details of his relationship with 'Daisy Renton' (how he ended it and how she reacted).	• 'And then you decided to keep her – as your mistress?' • 'I didn't feel about her as she felt about me.' • 'She was – very gallant – about it.'	The inequality in Gerald's relationship with 'Daisy' is clear, from his having the money to support her to her stronger feelings for him. This reinforces the themes of inequality in money, social class, and gender roles.
Eva called herself 'Mrs Birling' when she applied for aid from Sybil's charitable organisation.	Sybil thinks using the name 'Mrs Birling' 'was simply a piece of gross impertinence'.	Emphasises Sybil's attitude to women of Eva's social class and her lack of sympathy for her death.
Sybil takes no responsibility for Eva's death. She thinks whoever got her pregnant is responsible.	• 'Unlike the other three, I did nothing I'm ashamed of' • 'I blame the young man who was the father'	Priestley uses dramatic irony as Sybil is unaware of what is clear to the Inspector. Her insistence that the father is to blame will come back to haunt her when Eric is revealed to be the father. This links to the theme of responsibility.

Key terms — Make sure you can write a definition for these key terms

climax   conflict   convey   dialogue

Knowledge

Knowledge — PLOT

2 Act two

Turning points in Act two

Key turning point	Key quotations	Mood
Gerald and Sheila argue.	• Sheila: 'And if you'd really loved me, you couldn't have said that.'	The tense and angry mood at the beginning of Act 2 contrasts with the beginning of Act 1, and creates dramatic conflict with two previously united characters, now in opposition.
Gerald confesses that 'Daisy Renton' was his mistress.	• Gerald: 'She was young and pretty and warm hearted – and intensely grateful.'	This turning point shows that Gerald realises that he must now confess his relationship with Daisy, for which he expresses guilt and sorrow.
Sheila returns Gerald's ring.	• Sheila: 'You and I aren't the same people who sat down to dinner here.'	This indicates Sheila's newly discovered maturity and the fracturing of her relationship with Gerald. Priestley presents her as wiser than Gerald and her parents.
The Inspector turns his attention to Sybil.	• Inspector: 'But Mrs Birling spoke to and saw her only two weeks ago.' • Sheila: 'We all started like that – so confident, so pleased with ourselves until he began asking us questions.'	This indicates a change in mood, with Sybil far more in denial than Gerald was, and oblivious to much of the Inspector's power. Priestley shows the Inspector entrapping each member of the gathering.
Repeatedly, Sybil rejects responsibility, blaming Eva and the baby's father.	• Sybil: 'Go and look for the father of the child.' • Sybil: 'He should be made an example of.'	Sybil's anger and defiance increase the dramatic tension.
The Inspector repeats back Sybil's words to her; Sybil realises Eric is the father.	• Inspector: 'Make an example of the young man, eh?' • Sybil: (*agitated*) […] 'I *won't* believe it.'	Priestley's use of dialogue adds to the dramatic tension, leading to the climax of Act 2 and Sybil's realisation of her son's downfall.
Eric enters.	• '*extremely pale and distressed*'	Priestley brings Eric back, silent and upset, creating a change in mood from the previous explosive encounters. The lack of resolution creates a cliffhanger ending to the act.

> **REVISION TIP**
> Consider what changes at the turning points, such as Sybil's reaction when the questioning changes to focus on her.

> **LINK**
> The characters of Gerald and Sybil are explored in more detail in Characters on pages 34–39 and 52–57.

> **REVISION TIP**
> Consider how the turning points in this act influence your understanding of the characters. For example, Sybil attempts to maintain a superior attitude but is suddenly brought down to earth by the turning point realisation that Eric was the father she had been talking about.

> **REMEMBER**
> Eric's entrance at the end of Act 2 follows a similar pattern to Act 1, with Priestley ending an act with a cliffhanger. This could be discussed as one of the playwright's methods.

Retrieval

Answer the questions below. Cover the answers column with a piece of paper and write down as many answers as you can. Check and repeat.

Questions	Answers
1. What does Sheila return to Gerald?	The engagement ring
2. Who is described as 'hysterical'?	Sheila
3. Why does Gerald think Sheila wants to stay in the room?	To hear someone else 'put through it'
4. Which character is asked to leave the room, demonstrating society's attitudes towards gender roles?	Sheila
5. What important civic role did Arthur recently have?	The role of Lord Mayor
6. Who is revealed as drinking heavily?	Eric
7. Who was described as being 'gallant'?	Daisy/Eva
8. Which themes or ideas are reinforced by Gerald's ability to support Daisy as a mistress?	Inequality in gender roles, money, and social class
9. What name did Eva use when she approached the charitable committee?	'Mrs Birling'
10. Who says they 'won't believe it'?	Sybil
11. Who says they all started off 'so confident'?	Sheila
12. Sybil is on the committee for which charity?	Brumley Women's Charity Organisation
13. What dramatic effect is created by Eric's entrance at the end of the act?	A cliffhanger

Previous questions

Now go back and use these questions to check your knowledge of previous topics.

Questions	Answers
1. In what year is the play set?	1912
2. What prop does the Inspector show Arthur?	A photograph
3. Who does Sheila call 'a fool'?	Gerald

Now turn to page 104 and complete Practice questions 4–6.

Knowledge — PLOT

3 Act three

Key ideas in Act three

Key ideas	How methods are used to show these ideas
Social class and inequality	Priestley has previously shown that Arthur wishes to improve his social standing, so he is alarmed that his chance of a knighthood might slip away. This reinforces the idea of the insecurity of social standing, as shown in Eva's own descent into poverty and disgrace. In his final speech, the Inspector exhorts the Birlings to think about how their lives are all 'intertwined' and that they are responsible for helping others.
Family and relationships	After the Inspector leaves, Priestley highlights the divisions in the family by their different reactions to the possibility of it all being a 'hoax'. Arthur and Sybil are elated while Sheila and Eric remain disturbed. Sheila is not yet willing to take back Gerald's ring, a symbol of their relationship and her safe, wealthy life, showing that she has changed.
Money	Priestley shows Arthur's fixation on money by his reaction to Eric's admission of stealing money. Sybil is criticised for withholding her 'little bit of organized charity'. When Arthur says he'd give 'thousands' to put things right, the Inspector tells him he is offering 'money at the wrong time'. Money is a symbol of success, but also a metaphor for what the characters owe to others.
Responsibility and guilt	The Inspector's final speech uses **emotive language** to highlight the debt they all owe each other and the fearful cost if it is ignored. Eric confronts his father about his 'every man for himself' philosophy, representing the capitalist point of view.
Gender roles	The vulnerability of women in society is shown when Gerald suggests that the Inspector showed them all photographs of different girls, all of whom could have been victims. The difference between how Sibyl treats Gerald, who she believes is a hero for his cleverness, compared to how she dismisses Sheila, shows that the idea of male superiority is embedded in this society.
Generations	Priestly highlights the generational divide at the end of the play when Sheila and Eric, unlike their parents, are not ready to return to how they were before: Sheila says, '(bitterly) I suppose we're all nice people now'.

> **REVISION TIP**
> Practise using literary terms such as 'dialogue,' 'stage directions', or 'irony' in your writing.

> **LINK**
> To learn more about the themes of generations, responsibility, and money, look at Themes on pages 74–83 and 89–93.

> **LINK**
> You can read more about the use of emotive language in Methods on page 24.

Key events of Act three

- Act 3 begins exactly where Act 2 ended.
- Eric has entered the room and the other characters are staring at him.

- Eric, realising they all know what he has done, is bitter that his mother has made things worse.
- Eric says he met Eva when he was drunk at the Palace Bar.
- He 'threatened to make a row' and forced his way into her lodgings.

- Arthur insists that Sheila and Sybil leave the room.
- Eric admits that he had sex with Eva more than once and she became pregnant.
- Eric stole £50 from the family business to support Eva, but when she discovered that the money was stolen, she refused to take any more.
- Eric accuses his mother of killing his child and her grandchild when she turned down Eva's request for assistance.

- The Inspector says there are millions like Eva Smith and that we are all responsible for each other.
- After the Inspector leaves, the family argues about who is to blame.

- Gerald returns and says that there is no Inspector Goole, which Arthur confirms with a phone call.
- Gerald wonders if perhaps they were not all shown the same photograph and that perhaps each had an experience with a different girl.
- Gerald calls the infirmary and is told there hasn't been a suicide case there in months.

- Sheila and Eric continue to worry, while Arthur, very relieved, accuses them of being unable to take a joke.
- The telephone rings. Arthur is told that an inspector is coming to ask questions about a girl who has just died.

LINK
You can read more about structural elements such as climax, twists, and the handling of time in Methods on pages 20–21.

Knowledge — PLOT

3 Act three

The end of the play

The final act

- Relationships: Gerald and Sheila – no longer engaged
- Generations: division between the older and younger Birlings
- Important props: telephone, whisky decanter, engagement ring
- Emotions: Arthur, Sybil and Gerald: relieved, returning to normal
- Emotions: Sheila and Eric – 'frightened'; unsure of what to do next
- Twist: telephone call announcing that a girl has died and an inspector is coming

Final mood/stage image: sudden change – 'they stare guiltily and dumbfounded'.

The last moment in a play is important, as that will be the audience's final impression of the characters and raises the question of what will happen to them next.

While Priestley does not resolve what will happen to the family, there is a suggestion that there will be a price to pay for their past misdeeds.

> **REMEMBER**
> When exploring Priestley's methods as a writer, you could comment on how Priestley uses stagecraft such as plot twists and key props to create dramatic effects.

> **LINK**
> Generations, family, and relationships are further explored in Themes on pages 69–73 and 89–93.

> **REVISION TIP**
> When revising the play, remember to consider the stage directions as well as the dialogue.

What the audience learns in Act three

What we learn	Evidence	Effect on character/plot
More divisions appear between the members of the Birling family.	Eric says his mother 'hasn't made it any easier' for him. He accuses Sheila of being 'a sneak' for revealing his drinking. Arthur says Sheila doesn't have any 'loyalty'.	Priestley has stripped the genial social facade from the family. They are speaking their thoughts directly instead of hiding them under social conventions or subtext. The revelations of this evening have made the characters see each other differently. Sheila is accused of not standing united with other family members.
Eric admits that he forced himself on Eva, implying that he raped her, taking advantage of her vulnerability and poverty.	• 'she'd not had much to eat that day.' • 'I was in that state when a chap easily turns nasty – and I threatened to make a row.'	The themes of social class and gender are reinforced by the poverty in which Eva lived and her vulnerability. The brutality of Eric's actions contrasts with those of Gerald's, where there was at least some affection and care.
Eric has stolen money from the family business, which enrages his father.	Eric admits 'miserably' that he stole £50 'from the office.' Arthur is shocked and calls him a 'damned fool'.	Arthur's capitalistic outlook is emphasised when is he is arguably more shocked at Eric stealing his firm's money than he is about his behaviour with Eva.
Eric is disappointed in his father and angry at his mother.	He says his father is 'not the kind of father a chap could go to when he's in trouble'. He says his mother killed 'my child – your own grandchild'. He is 'almost threatening'.	The generational divide is shown when Eric turns his anger on his parents, lashing out at them with such venom that they may never be reconciled.
The Inspector urges the family to learn lessons from this evening.	'We don't live alone. We are members of one body. We are responsible for each other.'	Priestley reinforces these important ideas about class, money, and responsibility by the use of stagecraft: the Inspector silences the others, 'masterfully' takes the stage, delivers his emotive message, and exits to allow his words to sink in with both the characters and **audience**.
The characters' belief that the events of the evening were a hoax is suddenly proved mistaken and their relief is shortlived.	• 'And I must say, Gerald, you've argued very cleverly, and I'm most grateful.' • 'If it didn't end tragically, then that's lucky for us.' • 'That was the police.'	After the Inspector's exit, the characters experience a wide range of emotions, from blaming each other, to relief, to confusion and, finally, horror that they may have to go through it all again. Priestley's use of the time loop structure increases the power of the ending.

Key terms — Make sure you can write a definition for these key terms: audience, emotive language

Knowledge — PLOT

3 Act three

Turning points in Act three

Key turning point	Key quotations	Effect
Eric learns from Sheila that his mother has been blaming him.	• Sheila: 'Because mother's been busy blaming everything on the young man who got this girl into trouble'.	The mood is tense as the characters make bitter accusations against each other. This demonstrates a further deterioration in family relationships.
Arthur orders Sheila and Sybil out when details of Eric's behaviour emerge.	• Sybil: 'Oh – Eric – how could you?'	Priestley shows that Sybil is heartbroken at her realisation of Eric's actions. She is presented as subdued and crushed compared to her manner in Act 2.
To Arthur's alarm, Eric admits he has stolen money from the family business.	• Arthur: 'I've got to cover this up as soon as I can.'	Eric's theft evokes an angry and agitated reaction from Arthur as he focuses on the potential impact on the family's reputation.
Eric is furious at his mother for not helping Eva.	• Eric: 'She came to you to protect me – and you turned her away – yes, and you killed her'.	Priestley heightens the dramatic tension and conflict through Eric's anguished, emotional outbursts.
The Inspector sums up what has happened and warns that they must learn a lesson from this. He exits.	• Inspector: 'Stop! [...] And be quiet for a moment and listen to me.'	The Inspector's intentions are revealed to the shocked Birlings, whose reactions highlight their divisions.
Gerald returns and tells them that a police sergeant said there was no Inspector Goole.	• Sybil: 'Didn't I say I couldn't imagine a real police inspector talking like that to us?'	The mood dramatically changes when Gerald delivers what they believe to be good news. The elder Birlings are relieved and triumphant.
Gerald's telephone call to the infirmary confirms that no girl died by suicide that night. Sheila remains concerned, while Arthur celebrates.	• Sheila: 'I tell you – whoever that Inspector was, it was anything but a joke.' • Arthur: 'And they can't even take a joke.'	With this further confirmation, generational divisions are emphasised: the older Birlings are congratulatory and want to celebrate, while Sheila and Eric remain unsettled.
The telephone rings 'sharply': a girl has died and a police inspector is coming over.	• *'As they stare guiltily and dumbfounded'*.	The twist ending causes a dramatic reversal in mood, leaving the Birlings shocked, defeated, and confused, while the audience is left wondering what will happen next.

> **REMEMBER**
> Inspector Goole is a mysterious character and Priestley never entirely explains who or what he is. This adds to the play's unsettling ending.

> **REVISION TIP**
> While writing about a character, you may want to consider how they react to key turning points in the plot, for example, how quickly Arthur recovers when he believes it was all a hoax or how Sheila remains worried, despite pressure from others to forget all about it.

Retrieval

Answer the questions below. Cover the answers column with a piece of paper and write down as many answers as you can. Check and repeat.

Questions / Answers

#	Question	Answer
1	How did Eric force his way into Eva's lodgings?	He threatened to 'make a row'
2	Which character does Priestley present as being most fixated on money?	Arthur
3	Given the idea that women of their class should be protected, who does Arthur want to leave the room when Eric's story becomes embarrassing?	Sheila and Sybil
4	Who calls the infirmary?	Gerald
5	What prop does Gerald offer to Sheila?	An engagement ring
6	Who does Eric accuse of being 'a sneak'?	Sheila
7	What evidence did Eric have that Eva didn't have enough money?	She hadn't eaten much that day
8	Who does Arthur call 'a damned fool'?	Eric
9	Why does Eric say he didn't confide in his father?	He is 'not the kind of father a chap could go to when he's in trouble'
10	What structural effect is used at the end of the play?	A time loop
11	What is the effect of the Inspector's exit after his speech?	It gives the characters and audience a chance to reflect on the impact of what he has said
12	What are they told in the final telephone call?	That a girl has died and a police inspector is coming

Previous questions

Now go back and use these questions to check your knowledge of previous topics.

Questions / Answers

#	Question	Answer
1	Why did Arthur fire Eva?	She helped organise a strike
2	What name did Eva use when she approached the charitable committee?	'Mrs Birling'

✏️ **Now turn to pages 114–115 and complete Practice questions 28–30.**

Knowledge **METHODS**

4 Writer's methods

What are the writer's methods?

'Methods' refer to the ways a writer presents their ideas: anything they choose to do to show the story, characters, and ideas. This means the larger structural methods such as the big events of the text, their order, and how characters are used during the story. It also means the smaller aspects of text such as metaphor and language choices.

> **REVISION TIP**
> Learn the terminology for the methods Priestley uses to create meaning so that you can write confidently about them in the exam.

Handling of time

- *An Inspector Calls* occurs in continuous, unbroken time, which adds to the tension of the play. Each act picks up exactly where the previous one left off.
- With the events occurring in 'real time', the length of the play lasts a single evening for both the Birlings and the audience.
- The play ends with what might be considered a 'time loop', as the final phone call suggests that the play's events will repeat themselves.

> **REMEMBER**
> The twist ending cannot be explained logically but adds to the mystery of the play and reflects Priestley's interest in exploring how time works.

Form and structure

The **structure** of *An Inspector Calls* is a three-act drama, and it has elements of different **genres** of drama.

Genre	How this is used in *An Inspector Calls*
Drawing-room drama: a domestic-based play set in a single room	All three acts set in the dining room of the Birling home
A mystery/thriller: usually involves a detective trying to solve a crime	Inspector Goole arrives to discover who is responsible for Eva's death
A morality play: promotes a certain moral viewpoint; condemns sins	In Act 3, the Inspector explicitly states the moral of the play.
A **didactic** play: aims to educate the audience	The Inspector is designed to teach the characters and the audience a lesson about their responsibility to each other

> **REMEMBER**
> By setting the play in a single room, Priestley creates a claustrophobic environment, which increases the 'pressure-cooker' tension of the play.

> **REVISION TIP**
> You could consider how using the mystery genre helps Priestley deliver his moral message to the audience, for example, by keeping them intrigued as the Inspector reveals the Birlings' misdeeds.

Structure

Element of structure	Description	How it is used
Exposition	The establishing of the circumstances of the play.	Act 1: introduction to the Birling household. Celebration of Sheila and Gerald's engagement.
Inciting incident	What sets the drama in motion.	Act 1: arrival of Inspector Goole. Revelation that Eva Smith has died.
Conflict	When characters who want different things are put in opposition to each other. It can also be when a character experiences 'inner conflict'.	Acts 1, 2, 3: between the Inspector's beliefs and the Birlings'. Between the generations. Between Sheila and Gerald.
Complications or **rising action**	Additional revelations or actions which increase the intensity of the drama.	Acts 1, 2, 3: revelations of each of the Birlings' and Gerald's involvement in Eva's downfall.
Climax	The most intense moment of an act or play; usually occurs shortly before its resolution or ending.	Act 3: the Inspector's speech warning that they must change or face 'fire and blood and anguish'.
Falling action	Less intense section after climax, tying up loose ends.	Act 3: Gerald reveals there is no Inspector Goole and they believe it was all a hoax.
Cliffhanger	Occurs at the end of a scene or act and leaves the audience in a state of suspense, longing to know the outcome of the interrupted incident.	Act 1: the revelation of Gerald's involvement with Eva.
Twist	A surprising change, which turns previous assumptions on their head.	Act 3: a phone call reveals that a girl has died and they are to be questioned by an inspector.

> **REVISION TIP**
> Typically, a drama ends with a resolution, such as a marriage or a death, but Priestley deliberately leaves the play unresolved. Think about the effect of this.

> **REMEMBER**
> Each of the three acts has elements of this same structure, with revelations, conflict, and complications in each act. Each act reaches a climactic point and then ends suspensefully with an unresolved cliffhanger.

> **REVISION TIP**
> Consider how Priestley's structure decisions affect the play's effectiveness, such as revealing each person's guilt across the three acts rather than all at once, or the power of the suspenseful cliffhangers at the end of each act.

Knowledge — METHODS

4 Writer's methods

Setting, props, and lighting

Element	Effect
Set: dining room	Symbolises the wealth and comfort of this late Edwardian family. Presented as a pleasant home, but could imply the characters are trapped in it.
Prop: engagement ring	Symbolises the changing relationship between Gerald and Sheila.
Prop: whisky decanter	Used for celebration but also demonstrates Eric's need to drink.
Prop: telephone	Suddenly important in Act 3 as a connection to the outside world.
Lighting: changes – from *'pink and intimate'* to *'brighter and harder'*	Shows the effect of the Inspector's entrance and alters the mood of the play.

Entrances and exits

One of the demands of a single-set, continuous-action play is how the playwright manages the important entrances and exits of the characters.

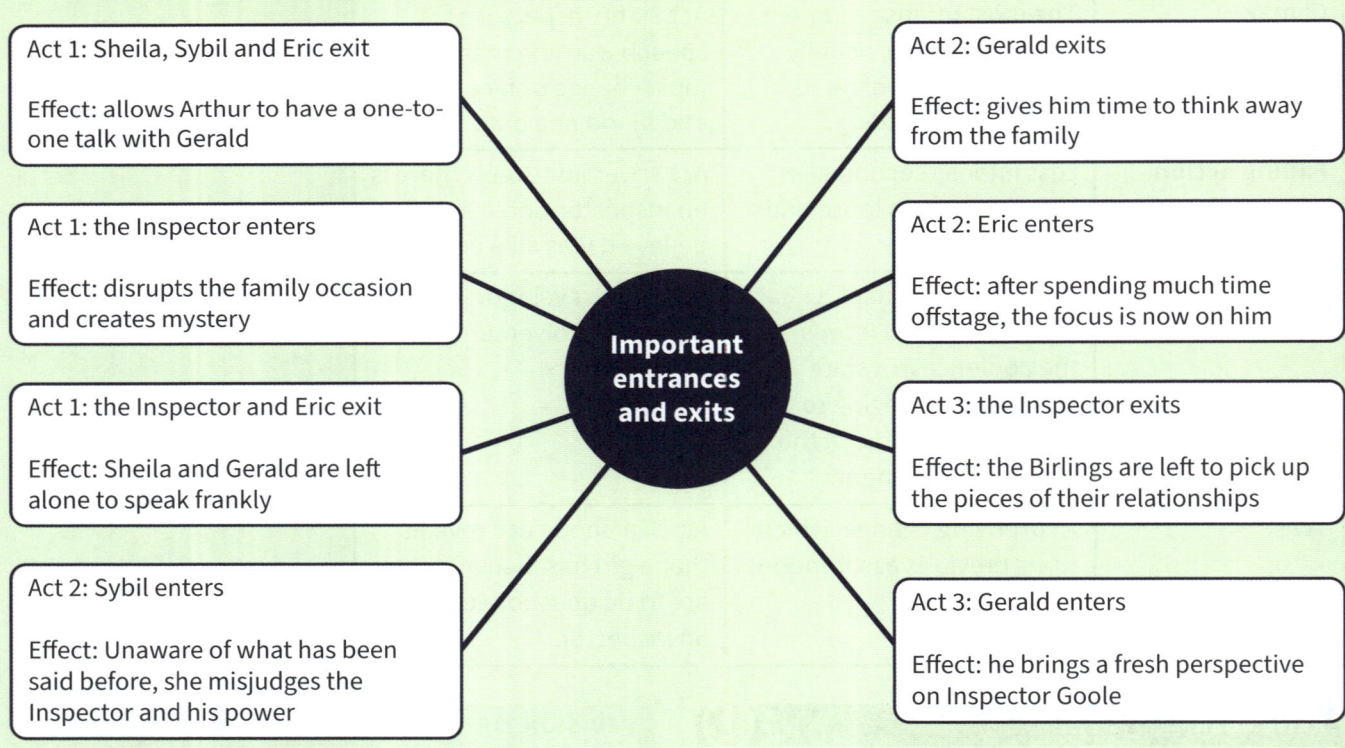

Act 1: Sheila, Sybil and Eric exit
Effect: allows Arthur to have a one-to-one talk with Gerald

Act 1: the Inspector enters
Effect: disrupts the family occasion and creates mystery

Act 1: the Inspector and Eric exit
Effect: Sheila and Gerald are left alone to speak frankly

Act 2: Sybil enters
Effect: Unaware of what has been said before, she misjudges the Inspector and his power

Act 2: Gerald exits
Effect: gives him time to think away from the family

Act 2: Eric enters
Effect: after spending much time offstage, the focus is now on him

Act 3: the Inspector exits
Effect: the Birlings are left to pick up the pieces of their relationships

Act 3: Gerald enters
Effect: he brings a fresh perspective on Inspector Goole

Stage directions

Priestley frequently notes how he wants a line to be spoken or an action performed. The **stage directions** help to reveal the characters and how they change throughout the play. Below are some examples of stage directions and what they might reveal.

Stage direction	What this reveals about a character
Eric: '*rather noisily*'	Compared to the other Birlings at the dining table, Eric is established as being disruptive.
Arthur: '*somewhat impatiently*'	Arthur is used to being in control and dislikes the Inspector taking the lead.
Sheila: '*with sudden alarm*'	Sheila is urgently aware of the danger they are in.
Inspector: '*taking charge, masterfully*'	Indicates a change in the Inspector's manner, leading up to his final speech.

> **LINK**
> You can read more about key stage directions and what they reveal about characters in Characters on pages 29, 35, 41, 47, 53, and 59.

Dialogue

The way in which Priestley writes the dialogue in the play often reveals a great deal about a character's background and attitude.

While much of the language used is formal, there are examples of informal language such as **slang** or **dialect**. Below are examples of informal language and what they might reveal.

Informal language	Type of informality	Purpose
Eric: 'Women are potty about' 'em. 'I think it's a dam' shame.'	'Potty' is slang for 'silly'. 'Dam' would be considered an expletive.	Demonstrates Eric's informality. Eric is pushing at the boundaries of what is socially acceptable.
Sheila: 'squiffy' 'Don't be an ass, Eric.'	Slang associated with the youth of the time.	Shows the casualness of Sheila's relationship with her brother.
Arthur: 'make 'em look prettier' 'clear out' 'Go on the streets?'	Informal dialect 'em' suggests casual speech or a regional dialect. 'on the streets' can be slang for being homeless or a sex worker.	Arthur's blunt language shows his lack of empathy and a certain brutality towards Eva. May hint at his background as a self-made man.

> **REMEMBER**
> There is a contrast between Gerald's easy formality and Arthur's more awkward choice of words and speechmaking.

Knowledge

Knowledge — METHODS

4 Writer's methods

Speeches

While much of the dialogue is made up of brief exchanges, there are a number of long speeches, often delivered at key moments in the play, particularly when a character is explaining their involvement with Eva Smith or when a character like the Inspector or Arthur wants to lecture others.

Priestley's dialogue is realistic and uses features of everyday speech, such as pauses, interruptions, and repetition. Below is an example of each.

Feature	Example	Effect
Pause	Act 1: Gerald twice 'does not reply' to Sheila when she asks if he was seeing Eva.	Suggests that Gerald cannot find the words to admit to Sheila what he has done.
Interruption	Act 2: Sheila interrupts her mother: 'Mother – stop – stop!' and 'But don't you see'.	Demonstrates how unstoppable Sybil is and her unwillingness to listen to Sheila.
Repetition	Act 3: Eric accuses his mother with the word 'killed' three times.	Shows how Eric, in his fury, is losing self-control and lashing out.

REMEMBER

Arthur, especially, is inclined to deliver long speeches offering the 'benefit' of his experience. This may suggest that he is used to commanding a room and being the centre of attention.

REVISION TIP

When thinking about speeches, consider that perhaps the most important interruption is when the Inspector shouts 'Stop!' before his final speeches.

Emotive language

Emotive language is used particularly by the Inspector as he tries to startle and shame the Birlings. Some examples are shown below.

Emotive language	Effect
Inspector: 'Burnt her inside out, of course.'	The shock and horror of these words jolt the characters out of their complacency and set up the tragedy of Eva's story.
Inspector: 'Just used her for the end of a stupid drunken evening, as if she was an animal, a thing, not a person.'	These words shame Eric, causing him to feel guilt for his abusive treatment of Eva, who was vulnerable due to living in poverty and her gender.
Inspector: 'if men will not learn that lesson, then they will be taught it in fire and blood and anguish.'	These vivid words inspire fear and alarm, alerting the characters and the audience to the dangers of the Birlings' and society's ill-fated path.

REVISION TIP

When writing about the author's methods, don't just name the technique but consider its effect.

Foreshadowing

Foreshadowing creates interest for the audience as they wait with anticipation for what will happen.

Quotation	What is foreshadowed?
Sheila: 'Yes – except for all last summer, when you never came near me.'	Finding out about the time when Gerald was involved with Eva/Daisy.
Arthur: 'so long as we behave ourselves, don't get into the police court or start a scandal – eh?'	The arrival of the police and the revelation of the family's scandals.
Arthur: 'Yes, you don't know what some of these boys get up to nowadays.'	That both Gerald and Eric have done shameful things.
Sheila: 'This isn't the time to pretend that Eric isn't used to drink.'	That Eric's heavy drinking contributed to his abuse of Eva and his subsequent theft.

Dramatic irony

Dramatic irony is when the audience or other characters know something that at least one other character does not.

Examples of dramatic irony	Effect
Act 1: Arthur: 'The Germans don't want war.'	The audience will be aware that the First World War broke out two years after the events of the play.
Act 2: Sybil's assertion that Eric isn't used to drink as he is 'only a boy'.	Gerald and Sheila are aware of Eric's heavy drinking and the audience will suspect it from various hints that Priestley has provided.
Act 3: Gerald: 'Everything's all right now.'	The audience and characters will shortly discover this is not true.

> **REMEMBER**
>
> Events of which the characters are unaware include the sinking of the *Titanic* in 1912 and the First World War which began in 1914. Priestley and his audience are aware of these, which creates dramatic irony.

> **REVISION TIP**
>
> When noting dramatic techniques make sure you also note the effect they have so that you can readily write about them in your exam.

Knowledge — METHODS

4 Writer's methods

Metaphor

An example of **metaphor** in the play is when the Inspector says 'We are members of one body' to suggest the connection between all of humanity.

Priestley also uses theatrical metaphor when something on stage represents something else.

- The Birlings' home: represents the comfortable upper middle class; a **microcosm** of late Edwardian society
- Eva Smith: represents all the ignored people living in poverty; the 'millions' of others whose specific stories we do not know

Theatrical metaphors

- Inspector Goole: represents society's conscience, a visitor from the future or Priestley's moral point of view

Tension

The play is full of tension, and, except for the play's opening, the mood is rarely relaxed. The tension accumulates in each act until all the characters are agitated and in conflict. Priestley uses various techniques for increasing this tension, such as:

- withholding information, such as only gradually revealing each character's relationship with Eva Smith
- changes in pace, such as the series of short, fragmented lines which lead up to Eric's slow, silent entrance at the end of Act 2
- conflict, such as the disputes between the different generations of the Birling family and between Sheila and Gerald, as well as the struggle for dominance between Arthur and the Inspector
- creation of high stakes, such as the audience's awareness that Arthur's hope of a knighthood, Gerald and Sheila's relationship, and the family's reputation could be destroyed by that evening's revelations.

REMEMBER
When a character is offstage, they do not know what is happening onstage. This adds dramatic tension when Sybil is unaware of the intensity of the Inspector's questioning of others and Eric does not know what his mother has been saying about Eva and the baby's father.

REVISION TIP
Think about the extent to which the characters are 'trapped' with the Inspector in the Birling home. This adds to the drama and tension of the play.

Key terms — Make sure you can write a definition for these key terms

complications dialect didactic dramatic irony falling action
genre inciting incident metaphor microcosm rising action
slang stage directions structure

Retrieval

Answer the questions below. Cover the answers column with a piece of paper and write down as many answers as you can. Check and repeat.

Questions / Answers

#	Question	Answer
1	What is the effect of setting the play in one room?	It creates a claustrophobic effect, increasing tension
2	How does the play fit into the mystery genre?	There is a detective solving a mystery
3	Whose entrance is the play's inciting incident?	The Inspector
4	What prop symbolises Gerald and Sheila's relationship?	The engagement ring
5	How does the lighting change when the Inspector enters?	It becomes 'brighter and harder'
6	Which character is inclined to make long speeches of advice?	Arthur
7	Which character's use of language shows what he is pushing at the boundaries of what is socially acceptable?	Eric
8	How is the generational divide explored through the younger characters' use of informal language?	Sybil disapproves of it, an early sign of tension between the generations
9	Which character makes particular use of emotive language?	The Inspector
10	What are hints about what will happen later in the play called?	Foreshadowing
11	What method is Priestley using when Arthur makes incorrect predictions?	Dramatic irony
12	The Birlings' home could be seen as a microcosm of what?	Late Edwardian society

Previous questions

Now go back and use these questions to check your knowledge of previous topics.

#	Question	Answer
1	Who does Eric accuse of being 'a sneak'?	Sheila
2	Who calls the infirmary?	Gerald

Now turn to pages 113–114 and complete Practice questions 25–27.

Knowledge — CHARACTERS

5 Arthur Birling

What we learn about Arthur Birling

Priestley establishes Arthur Birling as a self-satisfied capitalist, whose actions are contrary to the Inspector's (and Priestley's) socialist message. Arthur is the **patriarch** of the family. He is proud of taking care of his family and used to dominating situations. Sources of conflict include his tendency to assume a high **status**, his expectation that he will be obeyed, and the rigidity of his beliefs.

Arthur Birling

- **Predictions:** makes incorrect predictions about the *Titanic* and the unlikelihood of war – this use of dramatic irony shows Arthur to be a character who cannot be entirely trusted
- **Background:** '*rather provincial*', his social standing not as high as his wife's or the Crofts'
- **Occupation:** '*prosperous manufacturer*', employs many people
- **Interests:** was Lord Mayor, serves as a magistrate; plays golf with the Chief Constable
- **Goals:** to make his company more profitable; to gain a knighthood; to have Sheila make a socially advantageous marriage
- **Sources of conflict:** expects to dominate the Inspector; lectures the younger generation; is disappointed in Eric; is fearful of public scandal
- **Physical appearance:** '*heavy-looking*', '*middle fifties*', wearing '*tails and white tie*'
- **Relationships:** married to a '*rather cold*' woman; not close to son; has traditional ideas about the roles of women
- **Personality:** '*portentous*', self-confident, proud

Relationship with Eva Smith

Like each of the main characters, Arthur has a connection to Eva Smith.

Quotation	Effect
'A good worker too […] he was ready to promote her'	After initially denying he knew Eva, he reveals that he recalls her very well and that she initially made a positive impression.
'I told the girl to clear out, and she went.'	His harshness as a businessman is revealed as he not only refuses the raise but fires the 'ring-leaders' like Eva.
'The girl had been causing trouble in the works. I was quite justified.'	Arthur accepts no responsibility for Eva's death, believing he made a sound business decision and that it was all a long time ago.
'If you don't come down sharply on some of these people, they'd soon be asking for the earth.'	Arthur's treatment of Eva aligns with his belief that a man is only responsible for himself and his own family, while others must look after themselves.

How Arthur's character develops

Act 1:
- Generous host at a family celebration
- Tries to impress socially superior Gerald Croft
- Impatience with the Inspector for his intrusion
- Admits to firing Eva, but denies responsibility

Act 2:
- Becomes concerned about effect on family

Act 3:
- Tries to protect Sheila and Sybil from hearing more
- Conflict with Eric over him stealing the money
- Regrets possible scandal, says he would pay 'thousands'
- Resumes high status and jovial attitude when he thinks it was all a hoax
- 'Panic-stricken' at news that a girl has died

REVISION TIP

Pick six moments from the play that you think are important for understanding the character of Arthur and explain what you learn from each.

REMEMBER

Although Arthur goes through many emotional states, Priestley suggests that he has learned very little, if anything, as he is so relieved when he thinks it was a hoax. However, the final call implies he will eventually have to pay a price.

Key stage directions

Below are some of Arthur's key stage directions and what they reveal.

Stage direction	What it reveals
'noticing that Sheila is still admiring her ring'	He demands his family's attention before he launches into his speech.
'surprised'	He is caught off-guard when the Inspector doesn't agree about his refusing Eva a pay rise.
'with marked change of tone'	His attitude towards the Inspector changes when the Inspector indicates that Gerald, Eric, or Sheila may also have an involvement with Eva.
'puts the telephone down slowly and looks in a panic-stricken fashion at the others.'	Arthur's earlier confidence is gone as it dawns on him that their troubles are not over.

 **Make sure you can write a definition for these key terms**

patriarch   status

Knowledge

Knowledge — CHARACTERS

5 Arthur Birling

Key themes and ideas

Some of the key themes and ideas connected with Arthur, and the different methods used to present them are shown below.

Social class and inequality

Priestley shows that Arthur is wealthy, but Arthur's dialogue sometimes shows that he is uneasy about his social standing. He says Lady Croft thinks Gerald 'might have done better […] socially'. He hopes a knighthood would make him the Crofts' equal. While 'provincial' simply means that he comes from outside London, it can imply a lack of sophistication. Though Arthur may come from a humble background, he shows no desire to help others like him.

Family and relationships

Arthur is depicted as the leader of his family and frequently dominates. In Act 1, he dismisses Eric's 'public-school-and-varsity life' and in Act 3, says that he's 'spoilt'. In contrast, he treats Gerald with much more respect: 'You're just the kind of son-in-law I always wanted.'

Money

Arthur is preoccupied with money, and argues for 'lower costs and higher prices' even when toasting his daughter's engagement. When he finally regrets events the only way he can think to make amends is to pay 'thousands'.

Responsibility and guilt

Arthur states that a man has to 'look after himself – and his family too, of course' and dismisses people who argue for more social responsibility as 'cranks'. Priestley highlights Arthur's repeated unwillingness to see that Eva's death has anything to do with him.

Gender roles

Arthur expresses beliefs which were common at this time and in his social class, for example, that women need to be protected from harsh reality and that clothes are important to women's self-respect. He notes that Eva was a 'good-looking girl' and wonders if she ended up 'on the streets'.

Generations

Early in the play, there are signs of conflict with Eric such as when Arthur tells him to stop drinking and to 'just keep quiet'. This grows to full conflict when he blames Eric for the potential public scandal.

5

Writing about Arthur

Sample answer 1: not a strong answer

Here is an extract from a student response to this question, with the examiner's annotations and final comments. It receives less than half marks.

> How does Priestley present Arthur as an example of capitalism?
>
> [30 marks]
>
> AO4 [4 marks]

❶ This demonstrates an understanding of the text, but the methods that Priestley uses, such as stage directions, and their effect could be considered.

> Arthur Birling is shown to be a wealthy, well-dressed man who cares about his family. ❶ There are four members of the family, including two children and his wife, Sybil. The setting shows that he has money which is important in the play. He is also talks a lot about money, even when it isn't important. ❷ Arthur is used to dominating situations and makes a lot of incorrect predictions. However, on this night he is happy. He is used to getting his own way so is in conflict with the Inspector from his entrance onwards, especially about money. ❸ The Inspector is on the side of socialism because he thinks Arthur should have shared the money with the workers. However Arthur is all about the profits. ❹

❷ A clear textual reference is made but the effect should be explained and reference made to the question focus

❸ This shows an understanding of the text and correctly identifies conflict, but needs to connect this with the effect of Priestley's methods to characterise Arthur in relation to this theme.

❹ This shows a basic understanding of the conflict, but the final sentence is informally expressed and the idea of 'profits' could be more closely linked to the idea of capitalism.

Examiner's comments

In this answer, there is a general understanding of the character of Arthur Birling and the conflict between Arthur's beliefs and the Inspector's beliefs. However, the theme of 'capitalism' is not referenced, as the answer focuses more generally on money. The different attitudes towards the factory workers' strike are correctly cited to demonstrate Arthur's point of view, but the discussion of Arthur is rather general and, at times, off-topic. There needs to be a greater awareness of the methods Priestley uses to create Arthur as a character who represents capitalism and how Priestley develops the theme of capitalism throughout the play.

REMEMBER

To maintain the correct focus of your answer you could use some of the words of the question in your response.

Knowledge   31

Knowledge CHARACTERS

5 Arthur Birling

Sample answer 2: a strong answer

Here is an extract from a student response, with the examiner's annotations and final comments. It receives high marks.

> **REVISION TIP**
> Make a plan for how you would respond to this question, including what textual references you might include.

❶ A concise and accurate observation about Arthur's role within the play's context

❷ Uses some of the wording of the question and cites appropriate examples from the text to show the representation of capitalism

❸ Valid discussion of irony in terms of Arthur's incorrect predictions about the benefits of capitalism and their effect on the audience

❹ Chooses and analyses a relevant quotation relating to profits

❺ Connects observations to the theme of capitalism and introduces conflict and Priestley's message

Priestley presents Arthur as an example of a self-made man, with little understanding of wider social or political events or empathy for others, who is focused on his family and his company's profits. ❶ Priestley uses Arthur as an example of capitalism - from stage directions establishing the setting, showing how his family benefits from his business, to his transactional response to Sheila's engagement and his callous treatment of his workers in pursuit of profit. ❷ In Act 1, Priestley shows Arthur saying that capitalism will bring progress and peace, employing dramatic irony as the audience will be aware this is incorrect. This use of irony establishes Arthur as a character whose views on the benefits of capitalism should be questioned. ❸ Arthur is shown as obsessed with money. He views Sheila's marriage like a business merger, to bring 'lower costs and higher prices.' ❹ This puts him in conflict with the Inspector's (and Priestley's) beliefs about shared societal responsibility. Throughout the play, Priestley highlights the dangers of capitalism and this is shown through the downfall of the Birling family. ❺

Examiner's comments

The answer confidently addresses how Priestley establishes Arthur as an example of capitalism, including referencing Priestley's methods, such as stage directions and irony. Appropriate examples are used and focus on the question is maintained. In a longer answer, Arthur's treatment of the striking workers and the effects his choices have on others could be analysed further, as well as Priestley's warnings about the negative effects of capitalism.

Retrieval

Answer the questions below. Cover the answers column with a piece of paper and write down as many answers as you can. Check and repeat.

Questions | Answers

#	Question	Answer
1	What is Arthur's occupation?	Manufacturer
2	What is the importance of Arthur's incorrect predictions about the *Titanic* and war?	It lets the audience know that his other points of view cannot be trusted
3	What honour is Arthur hoping to receive?	A knighthood
4	How old is Arthur?	Middle fifties
5	What was Arthur's connection to Eva?	He was her employer
6	Who does Arthur tell to 'clear out'?	Eva Smith
7	Why did Arthur fire Eva?	She was a 'ring-leader' organising a strike
8	Complete the quotation: 'If you don't come down sharply on some of these people, they'd soon be asking for the _____.'	'If you don't come down sharply on some of these people, they'd soon be asking for the earth.'
9	Who does Arthur think a man needs to look after?	Himself and his family
10	How is Arthur's attitude described at the end of the play?	'Panic-stricken'
11	How does Priestley show that Arthur is disappointed in his son?	He says Eric is spoilt, and treats Gerald with more respect
12	Why does Arthur call people who argue for greater social responsibility 'cranks'?	He believes that a man has no responsibility for anyone other than himself and his family
13	What does Arthur believe capitalism will lead to?	Peace, prosperity, and progress everywhere

Previous questions

Now go back and use these questions to check your knowledge of previous topics.

Questions | Answers

#	Question	Answer
1	Which character is inclined to make long speeches of advice?	Arthur
2	How does the play fit in the mystery genre?	There is a detective solving a mystery

Now turn to page 103 and complete Practice question 1.

Knowledge — CHARACTERS

6 Sybil Birling

What we learn about Sybil Birling

Priestley depicts Sibyl as a representative of the comfortable upper middle class who feels little personal or societal responsibility to those who are not of her social class.

She is Arthur's wife, and mother to Sheila and Eric. She is presented as being accustomed to privilege. She is shown in conflict with the Inspector, who she views as an intruder, and with her own children, who react differently to the revelations about Eva Smith.

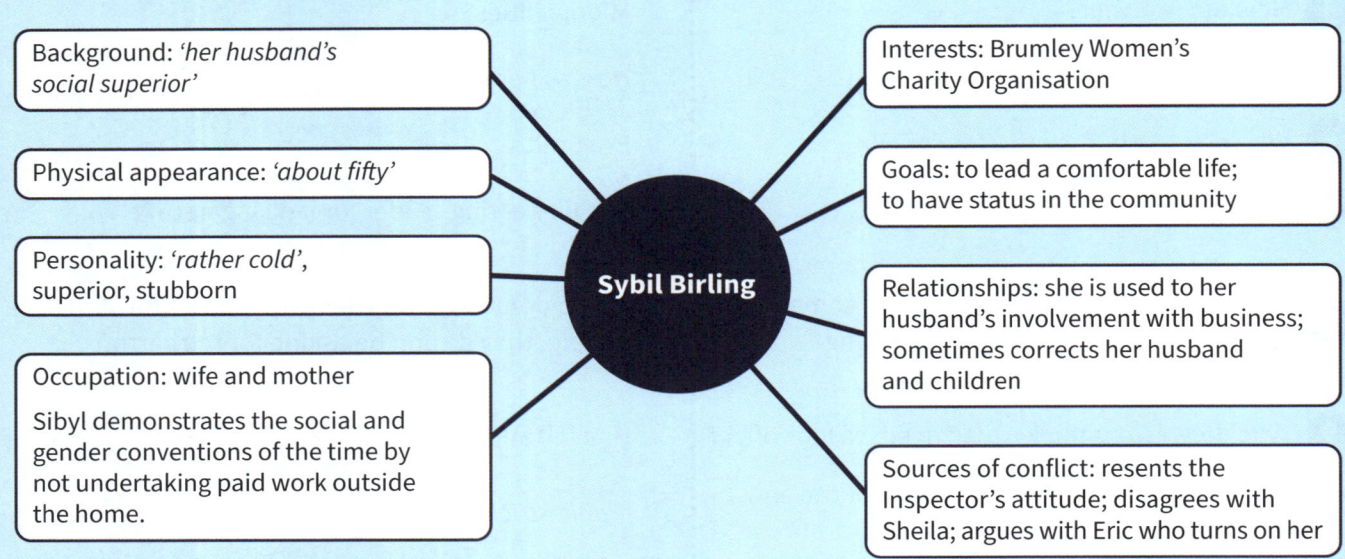

- **Background:** *'her husband's social superior'*
- **Physical appearance:** *'about fifty'*
- **Personality:** *'rather cold'*, superior, stubborn
- **Occupation:** wife and mother. Sibyl demonstrates the social and gender conventions of the time by not undertaking paid work outside the home.
- **Interests:** Brumley Women's Charity Organisation
- **Goals:** to lead a comfortable life; to have status in the community
- **Relationships:** she is used to her husband's involvement with business; sometimes corrects her husband and children
- **Sources of conflict:** resents the Inspector's attitude; disagrees with Sheila; argues with Eric who turns on her

Relationship with Eva Smith

Like each of the main characters, Sybil has a connection to Eva Smith.

Quotation	Effect
'We've done a great deal of useful work in helping deserving cases.'	When speaking about her work with the charity organisation, Sybil's use of the word 'deserving' is important as it shows that the committee is not just offering help but making judgements about the applicants.
'I didn't like her manner. She'd impertinently made use of our name.'	Sybil denies Eva assistance. Despite Eva's great need, for reasons of personal prejudice, Sybil influenced other committee members and turned her down.
'But I accept no blame for it at all.'	Sybil accepts no responsibility. She doesn't listen to the arguments that she could and should have helped.
'She was claiming elaborate fine feelings and scruples that were simply absurd in a girl in her position.'	Sybil shows a lack of empathy and judges Eva's social class as well as her being unmarried and pregnant. She only shows emotion when she realises Eric is the father.

6

How Sybil's character develops

Act 1:
- Hostess at engagement party

Act 2:
- Returns to dining room to encourage the Inspector to leave
- Shocked to learn of Gerald's affair with Eva
- Becomes focus of the Inspector's interrogation
- Blames Eva and the young man who got her pregnant
- Shocked to discover the young man responsible was Eric

Act 3:
- Conflict with Eric, who blames her for Eva's and the baby's death
- Grateful to Gerald for apparently proving it was a hoax
- Her relief and good humour are destroyed when she hears about the phone call

> **REMEMBER**
> At the end of the play Sybil, like Arthur, seems to want to dismiss the Inspector's visit as a bad joke and to resume her previous ways of thinking and behaving. However, the final phone call shows that she has more to learn.

Key stage directions

Below are some of Sybil's key stage directions and what they reveal.

Stage direction	What it reveals
'briskly and self-confidently'	Shows Sybil's lack of awareness of what has happened prior to her entrance and suggests she is entering to sort things out.
'rather grandly'	Shows the superior and patronising tone she attempts with the Inspector.
'exchanges a frightened glance with her husband'	After she realises what she has done, she turns to her husband for support.
'smiling'	Shows her relief at Gerald's apparent resolution of their problems.

Knowledge 35

Knowledge — CHARACTERS

6 Sybil Birling

Themes and ideas

Some of the key themes and ideas connected with Sybil, and the different methods used to present them are shown below.

Social class and inequality

As her husband's social superior, Sybil sometimes corrects others, for example, when Arthur praises the meal rather than waiting for the guest to do so or talks business on a social occasion. She chastises Eric for not toasting the couple and Sheila for speaking slang. She judges 'girls of that class' who get into trouble.

Family and relationships

Described as a '*rather cold*' woman, her relationship with her children does not seem close. She lacks insight into Eric, believing he's 'not the type' to be involved with Eva and, despite all the evidence, is in denial about his drinking. Within her marriage, she and Arthur fulfil conventional roles for that time.

Money

Sybil does not speak as directly about money as Arthur does. However, she enjoys the prestige that Arthur's prominence gives her and takes advantage of her influence with the committee women to withhold money from Eva. Also, she does not believe that a woman like Eva could have any scruples about taking stolen money.

Responsibility and guilt

Sybil steadfastly denies any responsibility or guilt even to the point of saying that 'Unlike the other three, I did nothing I'm ashamed of'. Later she is proud of being the only one who 'didn't give in' to the Inspector.

Gender roles

Sybil observes the conventional gender roles of the time, including leaving the men to speak together and attempting to shield Sheila from unpleasant conversations.

Generations

Sybil uses language which suggests that she sees Eric and Sheila as younger than they are, referring to Sheila as a 'child' and Eric as a 'boy'.

6

Writing about Sybil

Sample answer 1: not a strong answer

Here is an extract from a student response, with the examiner's annotations and final comments. It receives less than half marks.

> How far does Priestley present Sybil Birling as an unsympathetic character?
> **[30 marks]**
> **AO4 [4 marks]**

❶ Makes a relevant comment about Sybil's role in the play

❸ Uses two well-chosen quotations from stage directions which could be connected more clearly with how she is portrayed as unsympathetic

❺ Attempts to consider whether she is unsympathetic but needs to mention Priestley's methods

> Sybil Birling is as responsible for Eva Smith's death as anyone, yet her stubborn nature makes her unwilling to accept this. ❶ She is a proud woman who judges people who are from a different class than her and that made her prejudiced against Eva. ❷ Perhaps she is like this because she is described as being 'rather cold' and a 'social superior' to her husband. ❸ She spends a great deal of time offstage in Act 1, but in Act 2, there is more focus on her. ❹ She and the Inspector lock horns and, until the last seconds of the scene, she tries to blame everyone but herself. This makes her very unlikeable. ❺

❷ A sound understanding, but could explain methods used to show this or give an example from the text

❹ This is an interesting point, but the effect of this should be noted, such as that she is unaware of what has happened while she was offstage.

Examiner's comments

While expressing ideas about what might make Sybil an unsympathetic character and showing a sound understanding of her attitudes, this answer needs a greater sense of how Priestley achieves these effects, such as her dialogue and conflict with others. Some consideration could be given to what Sybil believes are the expectations of women at this time, as well as a connection to how Sibyl's attitudes towards social class and privilege add to her lack of empathy.

> **REVISION TIP**
>
> Make a bullet point list for how you would answer this question, including which textual references you would use.

Knowledge 37

Knowledge — CHARACTERS

6 Sybil Birling

Sample answer 2: a strong answer

Here is an extract from a student response, with examiner's annotations and final comments. It receives high marks.

① A confident opening with an acknowledgement of the context

To a great extent, Sybil Birling, is presented as an unsympathetic character, who lacks warmth, empathy, and insight. ① Described in the stage directions as 'rather cold,' she spends much of the first scene reprimanding others for their manners or speech. She confirms to the social conventions and gender roles of the time, leading her to withdraw with Sheila to allow the men to talk. ② In Act 2 that the full force of her superior and over-confident manner is revealed. As Priestley has her offstage for much of Act 1, when she re-enters in Act 2, her attitude is 'off-key' compared to the others who are aware of the Inspector's power and what has been revealed. ③ She speaks 'rather grandly' to the Inspector and tries to impress him with her husband's status because he was 'Lord Mayor only two years ago'. Here Priestley shows the limitations of her prejudices and ideas about social class. ④ Her most unsympathetic quality is her lack of empathy, particularly for Eva and women of her class. Her inability to grasp the complicity of her family in Eva's tragic downfall and her repeated ignoring of Sheila's desperate warnings make her shock and defeat all the greater. ⑤

② Mentions Priestley's use of stage directions, supported by observations of Sybil's interactions

③ Makes an observation about the effect of the structure of the play and uses a relevant quotation

④ Notes qualities that could be unsympathetic

⑤ Considers her worst characteristics and shows how Priestley heightens their effect

Examiner's comments

This response immediately addresses the question focus. It compares the presentation of Sybil in Act 1 with her more forceful and unsympathetic portrayal in Act 2. A longer answer could connect Sybil more thoroughly to Priestley's themes of social class and responsibility.

> **REMEMBER**
> Context refers to the circumstances revealed in the play and not external historical events.

Retrieval

Answer the questions below. Cover the answers column with a piece of paper and write down as many answers as you can. Check and repeat.

Questions | Answers

#	Question	Answer
1	To whom is Sybil said to be socially superior?	Her husband, Arthur
2	What committee does she serve on?	Brumley Women's Charity Organisation
3	Give two examples of how Sibyl observes the gender conventions of the time for women of her class.	Two from: she leaves the men to talk / she tries to shield Sheila from unpleasant conversations / she doesn't undertake paid work outside the home
4	Who particularly blames Sybil for the deaths of Eva and the baby?	Eric
5	Why did Sybil think Eva was impertinent?	She used the name 'Mrs Birling'
6	In which act does the Inspector accuse Sybil of being partly to blame for Eva's death?	Act 2
7	Who does Sybil congratulate for supposedly revealing the hoax?	Gerald
8	When does Sybil give a *'frightened glance'* at her husband?	When she realises she has accused Eric of bearing responsibility
9	What does Sybil criticise Arthur for discussing at the engagement dinner?	Business
10	Give an example of how Sibyl is presented as being unsympathetic by Priestley in her treatment of Eva.	She denies Eva charity money after making judgements about her as a woman of a lower class
11	Who does Sybil say she didn't give in to?	The Inspector

Previous questions

Now go back and use these questions to check your knowledge of previous topics.

Questions | Answers

#	Question	Answer
1	Which themes or ideas are reinforced by Gerald's ability to support Daisy as a mistress?	Inequality in gender roles, money, and social class
2	What honour is Arthur hoping to receive?	A knighthood

Now turn to pages 105–107 and answer Practice questions 9, 10 and 14.

Knowledge — CHARACTERS

7 Sheila Birling

What we learn about Sheila Birling

Sheila is the character who changes most in the play, from feeling 'very pleased' with herself to questioning her relationships and beliefs. Priestley presents Sheila as a representative of the younger generation who is willing to learn from her mistakes and is open to new ideas, including those radically different from her own upbringing.

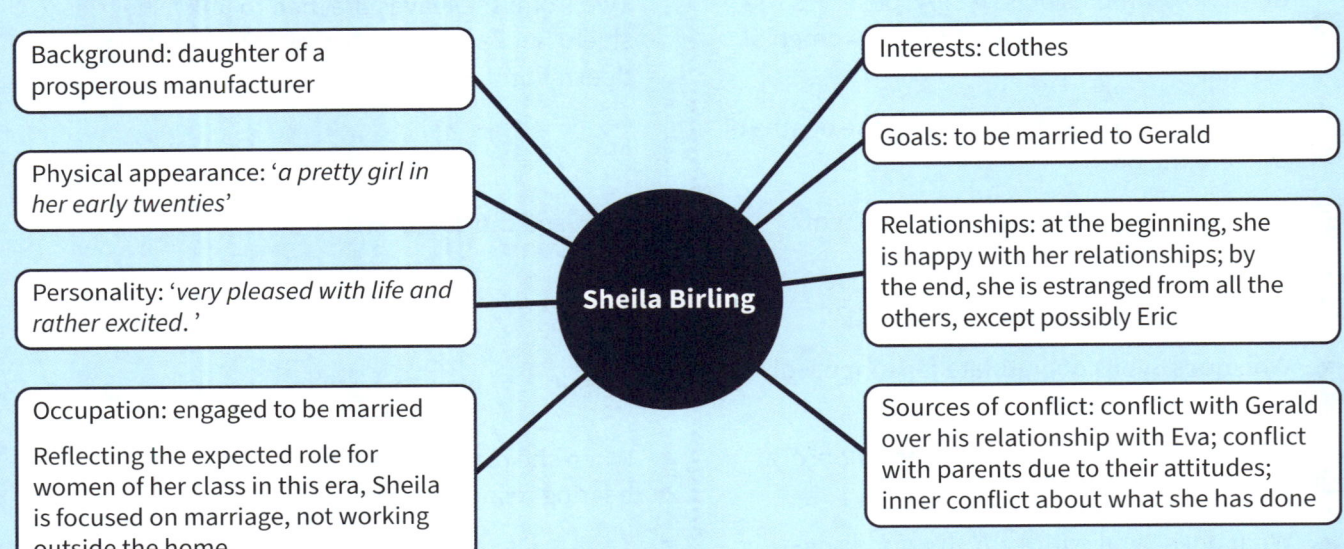

- Background: daughter of a prosperous manufacturer
- Physical appearance: '*a pretty girl in her early twenties*'
- Personality: '*very pleased with life and rather excited.*'
- Occupation: engaged to be married. Reflecting the expected role for women of her class in this era, Sheila is focused on marriage, not working outside the home.
- Interests: clothes
- Goals: to be married to Gerald
- Relationships: at the beginning, she is happy with her relationships; by the end, she is estranged from all the others, except possibly Eric
- Sources of conflict: conflict with Gerald over his relationship with Eva; conflict with parents due to their attitudes; inner conflict about what she has done

Relationship with Eva Smith

Like each of the main characters, Sheila has a connection to Eva Smith.

Quotation	Effect
'I caught sight of this girl smiling at Miss Francis – as if to say: "Doesn't she look awful" – and I was absolutely furious.'	Sheila's behaviour as a customer at Milwards reveals an insecurity about her own appearance and a jealousy of Eva's beauty. The word 'furious' suggests that she acted in anger rather than rationally.
'I went to the manager at Milwards and I told him that if they didn't get rid of that girl, I'd never go near the place again'	Sheila uses her knowledge of her family's powerful position as wealthy customers to wield her influence in getting Eva fired.
'It's the only time I've ever done anything like that, and I'll never, never do it again to anybody.'	Sheila immediately regrets her action, which was out of character for her, and vows to learn from it. Repetition of 'never' reinforces her sincerity.
'And I know I'm to blame […] I won't believe – it's simply my fault'	Sheila accepts her fault, but is also searching for larger, possibly societal, reasons for Eva's suicide.

How Sheila's character develops

Act 1:
- Delighted to be engaged to Gerald
- Sorry that Eva killed herself
- Discovers she got Eva fired
- Realises that Gerald knew Eva/Daisy Renton

Act 2:
- Argues with Gerald
- Breaks off engagement with Gerald
- Tries to stop Sybil repeatedly

Act 3:
- Is curious about the Inspector and his powers
- Cannot return to how she was before

> **REVISION TIP**
> Note the stage directions that Priestley uses to show the changes in Sheila's emotional state and practise using them when writing timed answers.

Key stage directions

Below are some of Sheila's key stage directions and what they reveal.

Stage direction	What it reveals
'half serious, half playful'	Shows that she is still somewhat bothered by Gerald's absence last summer, but disguises it with a playful tone.
'rather distressed'	Her naturally sympathetic nature is revealed by her reaction to Eva's death before she even knows of the family's involvement.
'laughs rather hysterically'	Reveals her high emotion and bitterness at realising more will be revealed about Gerald.
'tensely'	Her reaction to the supposed 'joke' contrasts to the light-heartedness of her parents and Gerald.

Knowledge

Knowledge — CHARACTERS

7 Sheila Birling

Themes and ideas

Some of the key themes and ideas connected with Sheila, and the different methods used to present them are shown below.

Social class and inequality

Priestley contrasts the lives of Eva and Sheila to highlight their inequality and the class advantages that Sheila has. Eva, with no family to support her and no money of her own, is reliant on low-paid work or the 'generosity' of men. On the other hand, Sheila doesn't need to work and will be supported by either her father or husband. She uses her class privilege to get Eva fired.

Family and relationships

At the beginning of the play, Sheila is shown to have a playful and affectionate relationship with Gerald and her family. She is delighted to be engaged to Gerald, which her family consider a very desirable match. Throughout the play, she becomes disillusioned with her family and frequently criticises them for their lack of a guilty conscience and insight.

Money

Sheila benefits from her father's wealth which allows her to move in socially acceptable circles and buy expensive clothes. She is also marrying into a family with money.

Responsibility and guilt

Unlike the other characters, Sheila immediately takes responsibility for her actions and is regretful, vowing to behave differently in the future. She also wants the others to realise their guilt.

Gender roles

Sheila conforms to the expected gender roles of the time for women of her class, such as prioritising marriage and not working outside the house. However, she stands up to her parents when they try to shield her from harsh realities and shows an independence of spirit. At the end, she is hesitant about agreeing to marry Gerald.

Generations

Priestley contrasts Sybil and Sheila, particularly in Act 2, where their very different reactions to Eva and girls 'of her class' are emphasised.

7

Writing about Sheila

Sample answer 1: not a strong answer

Here is an extract from a student response, with the examiner's annotations and final comments. It receives less than half marks.

> How does Priestley present Sheila's changing beliefs and attitudes in the play?
>
> [30 marks]
>
> AO4 [4 marks]

1 Accurately notes Sheila's initial mood and chooses an appropriate quotation. There is an opportunity here to look more precisely at Priestley's stage directions and other methods

3 Again accurate, but a more detailed or nuanced explanation of methods and effects is needed

Sheila is the Birlings' daughter and, at the beginning of the play, is shown to be very happy. She is delighted to be engaged to Gerald and receives the engagement ring with joy. She is 'very pleased with life and rather excited'. **1** Later in the play, the audience sees a more serious side to Sheila as she is sad that Eva has died and horrified when she learns that she played a part in her sorry end. **2** This shows that she has changed as her happy mood at the beginning of the play has changed to a sadder, more concerned one. **3** Unlike her parents, she is open to listening to the Inspector and learning from him. **4**

2 This is an accurate observation, but rather general. Could specify which attitudes and beliefs have changed.

4 This is an important point and provides an opportunity to contrast Sheila's changing beliefs with her parents'.

Examiner's comments

Although this answer shows a general understanding of Sheila and the play's plot, it needs more focus on Sheila's beliefs and attitudes, as well as the methods Priestley uses. For example: How do the stage directions describing Sheila's emotions change throughout the play? How does Priestley contrast her reactions to those of her parents'? How do her ideas about socialism and social class change throughout the play?

It is important to maintain a critical tone when writing and to remember that these are characters constructed by a writer.

> **REVISION TIP**
>
> Ensure that you know the difference between Sheila and Sybil and don't confuse them when writing.

Knowledge 43

Knowledge — CHARACTERS

7 Sheila Birling

Sample answer 2: a strong answer

Here is an extract from a student response, with examiner's annotations and final comments. It receives high marks.

> Sheila is the character who changes most dramatically in the play. In Act 1 she is playful and 'very pleased with life'. Priestley presents her as an optimistic, upper middle class young woman, who believes nothing could make her happier than to be engaged to Gerald. ❶ He implies that she's led a sheltered life as her parents frequently try to shield her from the Inspector's revelations by suggesting that she leave the room. ❷ When she learns of Eva's death, the stage directions show she is 'distressed', but tellingly, she asks if Eva was 'pretty'. This suggests the superficial nature of Sheila's beliefs, which change with the shock of realising her role in Eva's death. ❸ She, of all the characters, is most receptive to the Inspector's teachings about sharing responsibility. By the play's end, the family is fractured, with Sheila, in particular, not wanting to pretend 'everything's just as it was before'. ❹ The inspector says that the younger generation, for example, Shelia, are more impressionable. ❺

❶ Begins to answer question immediately and locates aspects of her beliefs and attitudes, such as belief in marriage and interest in pretty clothes, as well as an aspect of context

❷ Infers interesting point about Sheila frequently being protected by her parents

❸ An insightful close reading of the text showing how appearances are important to Sheila

❹ Identifies an aspect of the Inspector's teachings, which change Sheila's attitude

❺ Locates an example from the play that suggests why Sheila is more open to the Inspector's message

Examiner's comments

This answer identifies how Priestley presents Sheila, including his use of stage directions. The text analysis is sophisticated, inferring meaning from suggestions in dialogue. There is a clear example of a belief that has changed, supported by evidence from the text. In a longer answer, ideas about removing boundaries between social classes could be explored.

Retrieval

7

Answer the questions below. Cover the answers column with a piece of paper and write down as many answers as you can. Check and repeat.

Questions | Answers

#	Question	Answer
1	Priestley uses Sheila as a representative of what?	The younger generation who are more open to the Inspector's message of socialism
2	How does Sheila conform to the expected roles for women of her class in this era?	She doesn't work outside the home and is focused on making a good marriage
3	At which shop did she see Eva?	Milwards
4	What hint is given that she's insecure about her looks?	She has Eva fired because she is jealous and thinks Eva looks prettier than her and is smiling about it
5	How does she feel about getting Eva fired?	Immediately regretful
6	In Act 2, who does she repeatedly try to stop talking?	Sybil
7	To whom does she speak in a 'half serious, half playful' tone?	Gerald
8	What emotion does she feel when she learns of Eva's death?	Distress
9	Why is Gerald considered a desirable match for Sheila?	He comes from a wealthy family
10	How is her reaction to her involvement with Eva's death different to her parents'?	She accepts responsibility and they do not
11	Is Shelia still as enthusiastic about marrying Gerald at the end of the play?	No, she is hesitant
12	Priestley contrasts Sheila with Eva to highlight what important ideas?	Class inequality, and social and personal responsibility

Previous questions

Now go back and use these questions to check your knowledge of previous topics.

Questions | Answers

#	Question	Answer
1	Which character does Priestley present as being most fixated on money?	Arthur
2	In which act does the Inspector accuse Sybil of being partly to blame for Eva's death?	Act 2

> Now turn to pages 103–104 and answer Practice questions 3–4.

Knowledge — CHARACTERS

8 Eric Birling

What we learn about Eric Birling

Eric, at first, seems to be a light-hearted, if erratic, character, but is revealed to be a much more troubled character. Priestley establishes Eric as a damaged wayward member of the younger generation who is struggling to find his place in the world.

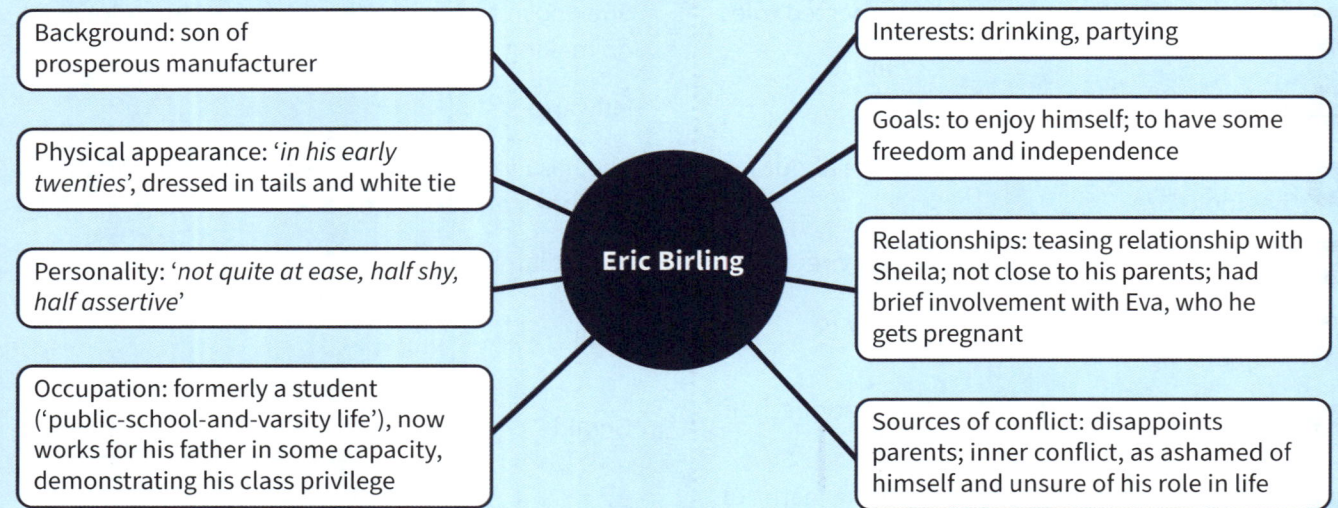

- Background: son of prosperous manufacturer
- Physical appearance: '*in his early twenties*', dressed in tails and white tie
- Personality: '*not quite at ease, half shy, half assertive*'
- Occupation: formerly a student ('public-school-and-varsity life'), now works for his father in some capacity, demonstrating his class privilege
- Interests: drinking, partying
- Goals: to enjoy himself; to have some freedom and independence
- Relationships: teasing relationship with Sheila; not close to his parents; had brief involvement with Eva, who he gets pregnant
- Sources of conflict: disappoints parents; inner conflict, as ashamed of himself and unsure of his role in life

Relationship with Eva Smith

Like each of the main characters, Eric has a connection to Eva Smith.

Quotation	Effect
'I'm not very clear about it, but afterwards she told me she didn't want me to go in'	This is the most shocking thing that Eric does – drunkenly forcing himself upon Eva, implying that he raped her. He has little regard for her feelings but says she is 'a good sport'. It is also revealing that his father appears more shocked by his stealing money than this.
'so I insisted on giving her enough money to keep her going – until she refused to take any more'	Eric gets Eva pregnant but is unable to support her. He attempts to take a degree of responsibility for his actions, but lacks the resources to do so. Eva doesn't want to ruin his life and honourably refuses his stolen money.
'Then – you killed her […] and the child she'd have had too – my child – your own grandchild – you killed them both'	The use of 'my' shows Eric's sense of responsibility for the pregnancy. This sense of ownership increases his fury at his mother, with 'your own grandchild' heightening the sense of connection between them and Eva's baby.
'You don't understand anything. You never did.'	Eric feels unable to confide in his parents. His use of the word 'never' suggests that there have been other instances when they didn't 'understand' him.

How Eric's character develops

Act 1:
- A playfully disruptive presence at engagement dinner
- Takes offence when Gerald jokes about him being up to something
- Is shocked at the news of Eva's death

Act 2:
- At end of Act 2, enters looking '*pale and distressed*'

Act 3:
- Admits to relationship with Eva
- Confesses to stealing money from the business
- Is angry and 'ashamed' of his parents
- Like Sheila, says he is frightened

> **REVISION TIP**
>
> Eric spends almost all of Act 2 offstage, only entering at the very end. This means that he is unaware of what has been said in his absence.

Key stage directions

Below are some of Eric's key stage directions and what they reveal.

Stage direction	What it reveals
'*suddenly guffaws. His parents look at him.*'	An early sign that Eric might be 'squiffy' (drunk) but also that his parents don't always approve of his behaviour.
'*who is uneasy, sharply*'	Indicates that Eric may feel guilty. Also, although he makes jokes, he doesn't like them at his expense.
'*His whole manner […] shows his familiarity with quick heavy drinking.*'	His handling of the whisky decanter is confirmation of earlier comments about Eric's heavy drinking. That he 'needs' a drink at this point suggests he may be an alcoholic.
'*almost threatening her*'	A shocking moment when his fury towards his mother hints at potential violence.

Knowledge — CHARACTERS

8 Eric Birling

Themes and ideas

Some of the key themes and ideas connected with Eric, and the different methods used to present them are shown below.

Social class and inequality

The family's wealth means that Eric has been educated and can rely on his family for money and work. His dismissive attitude towards the women at the Palace Bar indicates his sense of privilege.

Family and relationships

There are signs in Act 1 that his parents disapprove of him. By Act 3, their relationship is openly fractured. He has a superficially friendly and playful relationship with Sheila, but he feels she has betrayed him when she tells their mother about his drinking.

Money

Though Arthur says that Eric has 'more money to spend and time to spare' than he did when he was young, he doesn't have enough to support Eva. He steals £50 from the family business. Much of his money is possibly spent on drinks.

Responsibility and guilt

There are early signs that Eric feels uneasy and guilty, including his reaction to Gerald's joke that he might have been 'up to something'. He makes an attempt at assuming responsibility for Eva's baby, but doesn't see it through. He blames his mother for Eva and the baby's deaths.

Gender roles

Eric has stereotypical views of women, such as them being 'potty' about clothes. He says some of the women at the Palace Bar were 'fat old tarts', whereas Eva is pretty and 'a good sport'. He sexually assaults Eva and doesn't even learn her name.

Generations

Arthur thinks Eric has it 'easier' than he did. He is part of the younger generation who the Inspector thinks is more open to ideas about responsibility. The audience will know that young men like Eric would likely be called up to serve in the First World War, as was Priestley himself.

Writing about Eric

Sample answer 1: not a strong answer

Here is an extract from a student response, with the examiner's annotations and final comments. It receives less than half marks.

> How does Priestley present the characters of Eric and Arthur as contrasting?
>
> **[30 marks]**
>
> **AO4 [4 marks]**

❶ Answer begins with a contrast between the characters and accurately quotes from text

> While Arthur is presented as a 'portentous' man who sits heavily at the centre of his family, Eric is much more lightweight. Both characters drink a lot, but Arthur does not seem to be affected by his drink, whereas Eric is 'squiffy' and silly. ❶ The audience is given many clues that Eric may drink a lot and this becomes important later in the play. Arthur also drinks but there are not many signs that it changes his behaviour, except possibly making him more talkative. Another difference between Arthur and Eric is that Arthur expects Eric to listen to him, which Eric doesn't seem to want to do. ❷ By Act 3, Eric is possibly very drunk and behaving in a 'threatening' fashion towards his mother. ❸

❷ Identifies another difference, but this needs to be explored in more detail, perhaps discussing the differences in age and upbringing between the characters

❸ Makes a correct observation, but needs to look deeper into why Eric behaves this way and the methods Priestley uses

Examiner's comments

In this answer, several correct comparisons are made between the characters, such as their drinking and tendency to speak at length, but Priestley's methods of contrasting them needs to be explored in more depth, as well as the contextual differences between them, such as being from different generations. Insight into their different beliefs, such as their conflicting ideas about workers' rights, could also be discussed.

REVISION TIP

Priestley makes many references to Eric's drinking. Revise these references in the dialogue and stage directions, then write a paragraph explaining what this reveals about his character.

Knowledge — CHARACTERS

8 Eric Birling

Sample answer 2: a strong answer

Here is an extract from a student response, with examiner's annotations and final comments. It receives high marks.

> Priestley contrasts Arthur, a representative of the older generation, with his son, Eric, from the younger generation, and their different attitudes towards societal issues and money. ❶ While Arthur is a self-made man and therefore has the confidence that gives him, Eric is 'half shy, half assertive', with an erratic manner, who was born into very comfortable circumstances. This is clear in the first scene where Priestley has Eric puncturing the formality of the event with guffaws and silly jokes. ❷ When he does try to engage in a serious topic such as the prospect of war, he is interrupted by his father, who proceeds to lecture him at length. ❸ There is an irony to this because, unknown to them, as a young man, Eric is likely to be called up to serve in the war in two years' time, whereas Arthur is too old. ❹ Arthur repeatedly shows his lack of respect for Eric, saying that he has it easy, is 'spoilt' and doesn't seem to have learned much from his 'public-school-and-varsity life'. He contrasts this with his own days as a young man with little spare cash. ❺

❶ Connects question to one of the themes of the play, which could provide a useful basis for exploring Priestley's meaning

❷ Focuses in detail on clear example of contrasts and uses highly appropriate quotations and examples

❸ Looks at methods such as length of speeches and interruptions

❹ Notes 'irony,' an important Priestley method, and connects to context

❺ Well-chosen examples from text to highlight contrasts

Examiner's comments

A well-focused response with appropriate examples from the text. Priestley's methods, such as stage directions and irony are discussed, as well as the significance of the characters' different ages, given the context of the impending war.

Retrieval

Answer the questions below. Cover the answers column with a piece of paper and write down as many answers as you can. Check and repeat.

#	Questions	Answers
1	Give two examples of Eric's class privilege.	He is well-educated and has been given a job in his father's business
2	Who does Eric say is a 'good sport'?	Eva
3	Why doesn't Eva want to take the money he offers her?	She knows it is stolen and she doesn't want to ruin his life
4	Who does Eric blame for killing his child?	His mother
5	How much money does Eric steal?	£50
6	Where does he steal it from?	His father's business
7	He is offstage for almost all of which act?	Act 2
8	Who is he 'almost threatening' towards?	His mother
9	What joke does Gerald make that causes Eric to be uneasy?	That he might have been up to something scandalous
10	What does Eric say women are 'potty' about?	Clothes
11	How does Eric's treatment of Eva demonstrate their differences in class and gender?	He sexually assaults, and tries to give her money
12	What do Priestley's stage directions reveal about Eric's behaviour at the dinner table in Act 1?	That he may be drunk and that he behaves in a way that receives his parents' disapproval

Previous questions

Now go back and use these questions to check your knowledge of previous topics.

#	Questions	Answers
1	Who does Sybil congratulate for supposedly revealing the hoax?	Gerald
2	At which shop did Sheila see Eva?	Milwards

Now turn to page 105 and answer Practice questions 7–8.

Knowledge — CHARACTERS

9 Gerald Croft

What we learn about Gerald Croft

Priestley establishes Gerald Croft as a representative of a young capitalist who enjoys the advantages and freedom of his social class.

Gerald Croft

- **Background:** from an upper-class family; mother is 'Lady Croft' from an 'old country family – landed people'; family owns Crofts Limited, business rivals of the Birlings
- **Physical appearance:** *'an attractive chap about thirty,'* wearing tails and white tie
- **Personality:** *'rather too manly to be a dandy but very much the well-bred young man-about-town'*
- **Interests:** socialising around town
- **Occupation:** works for his family's company
- **Goals:** to marry Sheila and have a successful life
- **Relationships:** engaged to Sheila, but also was involved with Eva/Daisy who has greater feelings for him and became financially dependent on him
- **Sources of conflict:** Sheila calls off the engagement when his relationship with Eva/Daisy is revealed; possible damage to his and his family's reputations

Relationship with Eva Smith

Like each of the main characters, Gerald has a connection to Eva Smith (whom he knew as Daisy Renton).

Quotation	Effect
'She was young and pretty and warm hearted – and intensely grateful.'	The inequality of the relationship between Gerald and Daisy flattered him and gave him total control, including when to end it.
'So I broke it off definitely before I went.'	Daisy was not the kind of woman he could marry. Gerald ended their relationship at a time that was convenient for him.
'She didn't blame me at all. I wish to God she had now. Perhaps I'd feel better about it.'	He speaks of 'Daisy' with affection throughout. Her 'gallant' behaviour was better than he deserved.
'as I am rather more – upset – by this business than I probably appear to be'	He keeps his emotions to himself, not wanting to appear distressed in front of the Birlings, so goes out for a walk alone.

How Gerald's character develops

Act 1:
- Celebrating engagement to Sheila with her family
- Learns of Arthur's possible knighthood
- Hears of Eva's death but doesn't know that she's 'Daisy'
- Sides with Arthur's firing of Eva
- Learns that Sheila got Eva fired
- When he learns Eva became 'Daisy', he admits to knowing her

Act 2:
- He and Sheila argue
- Confesses relationship with Daisy and leaving her

Act 3:
- Returns from walk outside and says Inspector was an imposter
- Gerald thinks everything is all right and offers the ring to Sheila

> **REVISION TIP**
> Gerald is offstage for much of Act 3, missing the Inspector's speech warning the Birlings, and the revelations about Eric. This means that when he returns, his attitude is different from the Birlings'.

Key stage directions

Below are some of Gerald's key stage directions and what they reveal.

Stage direction	What it reveals
'*rather embarrassed, begins to murmur some dissent*'	The social awkwardness in Arthur bluntly commenting on Lady Croft's likely lack of enthusiasm for the engagement is demonstrated by Gerald's response.
'*nodding confidentially to Birling*'	Gerald is making a small joke at Eric's expense while also trying to ingratiate himself with his future father-in-law.
'*startled*' '*pulling himself together*'	Gerald attempts to hide his emotions at learning that Daisy was Eva and that she has died.
'*Holds up the ring.*'	Shows how Gerald is willing to pretend nothing has changed between Sheila and him.

Knowledge

Knowledge — CHARACTERS

9 Gerald Croft

Themes and ideas

Some of the key themes and ideas connected with Gerald, and the different methods used to present them are shown below.

Social class and inequality

Gerald represents the highest social class of the onstage characters. He has easy manners which do not come as naturally to Arthur or Eric. Although of a higher social standing than Sheila, it is a good match, whereas he did not consider marrying Eva, who would have been unacceptable. He admits 'I did keep a girl' as if she was a possession he could afford.

Family and relationships

His parents are notably absent from the engagement party, perhaps contributing to Arthur's feelings that Lady Croft does not approve of the match. He and Sheila have a warm relationship, but there are signs that she is possessive and jealous.

Money

Gerald is comfortably enough off that he could support Eva for months without having to resort to stealing money. He shares Arthur's capitalistic viewpoint as he agrees with Arthur's handling of the strike.

Responsibility and guilt

He expresses sadness at Daisy's death more than guilt. He sides with Arthur in his decision not to pay Eva higher wages. He is not included in the Inspector's warnings about the future, so the audience doesn't know his reaction to those warnings. However, once he has decided it was all a 'hoax' he wants to forget about it.

Gender roles

Priestley describes him as '*manly*'. Sheila says he is like a 'fairy prince' to Eva, meaning a high status man who saves a woman in distress. She also refers to him, sarcastically, as the story's 'hero'.

Generations

Like Eric, he would likely be called up to serve in the First World War in two years' time. However, unlike Eric and Sheila, he seems to side more with Arthur and Sybil Birling and wants things to return to the way they were.

Writing about Gerald

Sample answer 1: not a strong answer

Here is an extract from a student response, with the examiner's annotations and final comments. It receives less than half marks.

> How does Priestley use the character of Gerald Croft to explore the theme of inequality?
>
> [30 marks]
> AO4 [4 marks]

❶ Shows general understanding but doesn't directly connect to themes

Gerald Croft is from an upper-class family, which is made clear by Arthur's reference to Gerald's mother as 'Lady Croft' and her possibly not approving of him marrying Sheila. ❶ He is also well-dressed and used to the better things in life. By marrying Sheila, his wealth might increase as both families have successful businesses. ❷ Without thinking much about it, after picking up Daisy at the Palace Bar, Gerald takes advantage of his privilege by 'keeping' her, with no thought of how it will affect her later on. Although he seems fond of her, he also seems happy to forget about her. ❸ Instead he becomes engaged to Sheila who is more socially acceptable. He does not seem like an evil person, just unaware of what it's like for people who don't have his advantages. ❹

❷ Again, while not inaccurate, this doesn't address methods or theme directly.

❸ This observation could be supported by detail from the text.

❹ This is a reasonable personal response but needs to be supported by evidence from the text.

Examiner's comments

This answer would be improved by a greater awareness that Gerald is a construction of Priestley's rather than a real person, and by identifying clearly what theme is being explored. It is important to pinpoint the methods Priestley uses to explore themes, such as contrasting Gerald with the Birlings and with Eva/Daisy.

REVISION TIP

Create a mind map plan for how you would answer this question.

Knowledge 55

Knowledge — CHARACTERS

9 Gerald Croft

Sample answer 2

Here is an extract from a student response, with examiner's annotations and final comments. It receives high marks.

> A key theme of 'An Inspector Calls' is inequality. This inequality is demonstrated by the different advantages available to middle- and upper-class characters, like the Birlings and Gerald, as compared to the few opportunities offered to Eva Smith. ❶ Gerald is established in the opening stage directions as a 'well-bred' young Edwardian gentleman, who works, but also has ample time and money for socialising, as expected of a 'man-about-town'. ❷ The Birlings cannot hide their delight that Sheila is making such an advantageous marriage, and try to impress Gerald by hinting that Arthur may receive a knighthood, making them closer to social equals. ❸ However, the dark side of the play's inequality is exposed in his relationship with Eva/Daisy, who becomes totally dependent on him. Despite expressing affection for her, he is no 'fairy prince' (as Sheila sarcastically says) as he has no intention of spoiling his social status by marrying her. ❹ Priestley demonstrates that inequality is at the heart of their relationship in terms of social class, money and affection. ❺

❶ Starts with clear understanding of Priestley's presentation of theme of inequality

❷ Considers in detail how Priestley uses stage directions to show Gerald's advantages

❸ Shows insight into the unequal social status between the Birlings and the Crofts

❹ Analyses the inequality between Daisy and Gerald

❺ Concisely sums up different types of inequality

Examiner's comments

This answer confidently chooses appropriate examples of inequality in the play and the important role Gerald plays in Priestley's presentation of this theme. There is nuance in the discussion, suggesting that Gerald is behaving in a socially conventional way for the time, rather than intending to cause harm. In a longer answer, aspects of the inequality theme, such as Priestley's attitudes about socialism as opposed to Gerald Croft's capitalistic viewpoint, could be explored.

Retrieval

Answer the questions below. Cover the answers column with a piece of paper and write down as many answers as you can. Check and repeat.

Questions | Answers

#	Question	Answer
1	How old is Gerald?	About thirty
2	Give two examples of the inequality in Gerald and Daisy's relationship.	She becomes financially dependent upon him; she has greater feelings for him
3	Who does Gerald say was 'gallant'?	Daisy/Eva
4	With whom does Gerald argue at the beginning of Act 2?	Sheila
5	What does Gerald offer Sheila at the end of the play?	The engagement ring
6	What important themes does Priestley explore in Gerald's contrasting relationships with Sheila and Daisy?	Social class, money, and gender roles
7	How does Gerald briefly react when he learns that Eva was Daisy?	He was startled
8	With whom does Gerald side about not paying higher wages?	Arthur
9	What fairytale character does Sheila compare Gerald to?	A fairy prince
10	Where did Gerald meet Daisy?	The Palace Bar
11	How does Priestley show that Gerald's views are more capitalist than socialist?	He sides with Arthur's handling of the strike

Previous questions

Now go back and use these questions to check your knowledge of previous topics.

Questions | Answers

#	Question	Answer
1	In Act 1, which character does Priestley present as dominating the dialogue, showing his comfort in his role in society?	Arthur
2	Eric is offstage for almost all of which act?	Act 2

Now turn to page 103 and answer Practice question 2.

Knowledge — CHARACTERS

10 Inspector Goole

What we learn about Inspector Goole

Inspector Goole is a mysterious character and it is debatable to what extent he is a realistic or symbolic character. His entrance is the play's inciting incident, setting off the chain of revelations. Priestley uses Goole as an advocate for his socialist message of social responsibility.

Inspector Goole

- Background: as a police inspector, he is presumably lower middle class; the name 'Goole' may suggest that he is a mysterious figure, such as a ghost or ghoul
- Relationships: unknown
- Personality: '*need not be a big man but he creates at once an impression of massiveness, solidity and purposefulness*'
- Occupation: police inspector
- Interests: politics and justice; doesn't drink on duty, or play golf
- Goals: justice for Eva Smith and others like her; to teach the Birlings their responsibilities
- Physical appearance: '*in his fifties, dressed in a plain darkish suit of the period*'
- Sources of conflict: conflict between his beliefs and those of the Birlings

Relationship with Eva Smith

Quotation	Effect
'I've been round to the room she had, and she'd left a letter there and a sort of diary.'	It is implied that the information the Inspector found in her room led him to investigating the Birlings and Gerald.
'She wasn't pretty when I saw her today, but she had been pretty – very pretty.'	Eva's prettiness is mentioned many times in the play and adds to the pitiful quality of her horrible death.
'if sometimes we tried to put ourselves in the place of these young women counting their pennies'	Throughout the play, the Inspector is encouraging the Birlings to feel **empathy** rather than separate from others who are less fortunate.
'One Eva Smith has gone – but there are millions and millions of Eva Smiths and John Smiths still left'	Key to the Inspector's message is that Eva is not a lone case, but just one example of those with whom the Birlings should realise their lives are intertwined.

Key terms — Make sure you can write a definition for this key term: *empathy*

How Inspector Goole's character develops

Act 1:
- Enters the Birling household to investigate Eva's death
- Forcefully questions Arthur about firing Eva
- Shames Sheila about her treatment of Eva
- Shocks Gerald by saying Eva became 'Daisy'

Act 2:
- Conflict with Sybil who patronises him
- Draws out Gerald's relationship with Daisy
- Forces Sybil to admit she turned Eva down

Act 3:
- Questions Eric harshly about his relationship with Eva
- Passionately lectures the Birlings on their social responsibility

> **REMEMBER**
> While the Inspector reveals most of Eva's life chronologically, he reverses the order of Sybil's meeting with her, which was the most recent, with Eric's, causing a greater sense of surprise when Eric's role is revealed.

Key stage directions

Below are some of the Inspector's key stage directions and what they reveal.

Stage direction	What it reveals
'dryly'	Suggests he sees the absurdity of Arthur trying to impress him by saying he plays golf with the Chief Constable.
'He regards her calmly while she stares at him wonderingly and dubiously.'	This shows how the Inspector isn't impressed by Sybil's sense of superiority and how she is confused by his refusal to submit to her wishes.
'massively'	A word that Priestley uses in relation to the Inspector which suggests his presence and impact on others.
'taking charge, masterfully'	Before his final speeches, the Inspector dramatically takes centre stage and delivers his message.

> **REMEMBER**
> Although focused and intense throughout, the Inspector becomes particularly forceful in Act 3.

Knowledge — CHARACTERS

10 Inspector Goole

Themes and ideas

Some of the key themes and ideas connected with Inspector Goole, and the different methods used to present them are shown below.

Social class and inequality

Arthur says that the Inspector is 'probably a Socialist or some sort of crank'. However, the Inspector's belief in socialism aligns with his desire for shared responsibility. He encourages the Birlings to see their lives intertwined with the working classes.

Family and relationships

The Inspector is not shown to have any personal relationships but has taken a great interest in trying to understand Eva, including visiting her room and reading her letter and diary. He shows great empathy towards her.

Money

The Inspector's attitude towards money contrasts with Arthur's. While Arthur argues the capitalist point of view, the Inspector promotes a socialist argument, for example, being sympathetic with the striking factory workers: 'But after all it's better to ask for the earth than to take it.'

Responsibility and guilt

The Inspector's persistent questioning and use of emotive language increases the sense of guilt, particularly in the younger characters. He declares in his final speech: 'We are members of one body. We are responsible for each other.'

Gender roles

He expresses sympathy for working-class girls like Eva and draws out the difficulties of their lives without judging them.

Generations

He feels he has more chance of reaching the younger generation: 'They're more impressionable.'

> **REMEMBER**
> The Inspector is sometimes considered a metaphor, for example, for society's conscience, rather than a realistic character.

Writing about Inspector Goole

Sample answer 1: not a strong answer

Here is an extract from a student response, with the examiner's annotations and final comments. It receives less than half marks.

> How does Priestley use the Inspector to challenge the Birlings' beliefs?
>
> [30 marks]
>
> AO4 [4 marks]

❶ A rather informal opening sentence, which doesn't directly address the question.

❸ This is accurate, but needs to show which beliefs of the Birlings are being challenged.

> It is hard to know what to make of the Inspector character as he might not even be real. His name, Goole, might mean that he is a ghost or a figment of the Birlings' guilty consciences. ❶ He certainly changes the mood of the play which goes from one of celebration to a police investigation. One way that he challenges the Birlings is by not playing by their rules. ❷ He refuses to let Arthur or Sybil take charge and he uses harsh language with Sheila and Eric. He rarely softens his blow. One example of this is when he accuses Eric of treating Eva like 'an animal'. This would challenge their beliefs as this is not how they previously thought of Eric. ❸ Another way he challenges them is when he silences them and delivers his speech about all being 'members of one body'. This would challenge their beliefs because they believe everyone should look after themselves and aren't responsible for people outside their own family. ❹

❷ This is true, but doesn't establish what beliefs of the Birlings are being challenged.

❹ A well-chosen quotation with the beginning of a good analysis of what beliefs the Inspector is challenging, but this needs to be developed.

Examiner's comments

This response would benefit from a clearer organisation of ideas. For example, the Inspector's name is not a strong way to begin an answer about how he challenges the Birlings' belief. A discussion of ideas, such as those about capitalism and social class, as well as the methods Priestley uses to present these ideas would have been more relevant.

REVISION TIP

Make a bullet point list of ideas and textual references you would include in an answer to this question, then number them in order of importance.

Knowledge — CHARACTERS

10 Inspector Goole

Sample answer 2: a strong answer

Here is an extract from a student response, with examiner's annotations and final comments. It receives high marks.

> Priestley uses Inspector Goole as a catalyst for change through his challenging of the Birlings' beliefs about capitalism, social privilege and maintaining the status quo. His entrance is the inciting incident of the play launching the plot into motion. ❶ Presenting Eva as a representative for all misused working-class girls, and using emotive language – 'Burnt her inside out' – to shock them, the Inspector exposes the flaws in the Birlings' beliefs. ❷ For example, Arthur's belief that profit is all-important is challenged by the Inspector's exposure of the effect that being fired had on Eva's life. Sibyl's ideas about social class and family are challenged when she learns that she refused help to the mother of her own grandchild. Sheila discovers that she and Gerald are not the simple, perfect match that she imagined. ❸ Sheila feels they are so altered by the Inspector's revelations, that they 'aren't the same people who sat down to dinner.' ❹ To heighten this sense of their beliefs crumbling, Priestley uses stage directions, which at the beginning show the Birling's as comfortable and united, but which change at the end to show they are in conflict. ❺

❶ Demonstrates understanding of dramatic situation and techniques, and references the Birlings' beliefs

❷ Demonstrates understanding of what Eva represents, and notes the effect of emotive language

❸ Pinpoints and explains the Birlings' beliefs and how the Inspector has challenged them

❹ Uses an accurate textual reference showing how Sheila has changed after being challenged

❺ Perceptive analysis of Priestley's method of using stage directions to show how the Birlings have changed

Examiner's comments

This answer demonstrates skill in choosing key moments from the play to analyse. In a longer answer the Inspector's message later in the play could be discussed, as well as the mystery of the ending, which suggests further challenges for the Birlings.

Retrieval 10

Answer the questions below. Cover the answers column with a piece of paper and write down as many answers as you can. Check and repeat.

#	Questions	Answers
1	What is the inciting incident of the play?	The Inspector's entrance and announcement of Eva's death
2	The Inspector's name sounds like what word suggesting a ghost?	Ghoul
3	What is the Inspector's goal in the play?	Justice for Eva Smith and people like her
4	How old is the Inspector?	In his fifties
5	What stage direction does Priestley use to suggest his stage presence?	*'massiveness'*
6	In which act does the Inspector deliver his warning speech to the Birlings?	Act 3
7	What stage directions does Priestley use to show the importance of the Inspector's final speeches?	*'taking charge, masterfully'*
8	How does the Inspector know so much about Eva?	He has read her letter and diary
9	What political view does the Inspector represent?	Socialist
10	What is the importance of the Inspector's statement 'But after all it's better to ask for the earth than to take it'?	It shows his sympathy for the strikers rather than the factory owners
11	Why does the Inspector think he does better reaching the younger generation?	He believes they are more impressionable
12	Who does the Inspector accuse of treating Eva like an animal?	Eric

Previous questions

Now go back and use these questions to check your knowledge of previous topics.

#	Questions	Answers
1	With whom does Gerald argue at the beginning of Act 2?	Sheila
2	Where did Gerald meet Daisy?	At the Palace Bar

Now turn to page 104 and answer Practice questions 5–6.

Knowledge — THEMES

11 Social class and inequality

Social classes in Edwardian England

The late Edwardian setting is a powerful one for exploring social class.

- This period, was a time of great prosperity for Britain, but there were also extreme inequalities in the distribution of wealth.
- The upper and middle classes controlled most of the wealth, while the lives of the working classes were far more precarious.
- Poor single mothers were often considered the lowest of social classes. Without a husband to support them, usually unable to find work and often socially shunned, they were often be dependent on charity for their survival.

> **REMEMBER**
> You do not need to include dates and historical information in your answer. Contextual information should always relate to the question.

> **REVISION TIP**
> Make a bullet point list of comparisons between social classes, then number the points in order according to your sense of their importance.

How does Priestley establish social class?

Ways of establishing social class

- **Described in dialogue:**
  - upper – 'landed people', 'royalty visited'
  - lower – 'miserable back room', 'They'd be all broke'

- **Setting:**
  - upper middle class – *'fairly large suburban house'*

- **Occupations:**
  - upper and upper middle class – manufacturers (Birlings, Crofts)
  - working class – servant (Edna), factory worker/shop assistant (Eva)

- **Hobbies:**
  - upper middle class – golf (Arthur), man-about-town (Gerald), buying clothes (Sheila)

- **Contrasts:**
  - the abundance of food and drink at the Birlings' home contrasts with Eva's hunger
  - the Birlings seated while Edna waits on them
  - Sheila buying clothes versus Eva working in a clothing shop

- **Crossing class boundaries:**
  - both Gerald and Eric socialise at the Palace Bar where men of their class can meet working-class women

64   11 Social class and inequality

Fluidity of social class

Priestley suggests that there are instances where a character's social status might rise or fall.

- Arthur improves his social status through his marriage and wealth, and a knighthood would raise him further.
- Eva's job at Milwards is a lucky break for her and a step up from the factory, but she is then shown to drop from employed working class to poverty when she loses her job and becomes pregnant.

> **REMEMBER**
>
> When writing about theme, remember literary devices that the playwright uses to convey the theme.

Quotation	What this tells us
'her husband's social superior'	Arthur has married a woman of a higher social class than himself, which, combined with his income, would further raise his social standing.
'You're just the kind of son-in-law I always wanted.'	Arthur is pleased that Sheila's marriage to a prosperous man will consolidate both their business and social standing.
'public-school-and-varsity life'	Arthur has provided Eric with what is probably a higher standard of education than he had, which could ease his entry into an upper social circle.
'when this comes out at the inquest, it isn't going to do us much good.'	Arthur realises the scandal of their involvement with Eva's death could cost him his hoped-for knighthood and ruin their reputations.

Use of metaphor

> 'One Eva Smith has gone – but there are millions and millions and millions of Eva Smiths and John Smiths still left with us'

Eva Smith serves as a metaphor, representing all struggling working-class women. The commonness of her last name, 'Smith', gives her an 'everywoman' quality. She later changes her name to 'Daisy' which suggests a pretty, but common, flower, appropriate perhaps because her prettiness is what is noted by others. Later, Eric admits he doesn't know her name and Eva gives a false name to Sybil, suggesting a further sense of loss of identity as her social standing descends.

Priestley uses another metaphor when Sheila says the Birlings mustn't consider there is 'a kind of wall' which exists between them and girls like Eva. This is the metaphoric boundary the Inspector wants to break down.

> **LINK**
>
> For more on Sheila and Eva, look back at Characters on pages 40–45.

Knowledge — THEMES

11 Social class and inequality

Writing about social class and inequality

Sample answer 1: not a strong answer

Here is an extract from a student response, with the examiner's annotations and final comments. It receives less than half marks.

> How does Priestley use the characters Sheila and Eva to present inequality?
>
> **[30 marks]**
> **AO4 [4 marks]**

In some ways, Sheila and Eva have a lot in common, as they are similar ages and both have relationships with Gerald. ❶ However, it is hard to have a complete picture of Eva as she is reportedly dead before the start of the play and we only hear her talked about by others. We never hear her own words. On the other hand, Sheila has one of the largest roles in the play, so we get to know a lot about her. ❷ One thing is that she is happy to be engaged to Gerald and gets a beautiful engagement ring from him. She also likes pretty clothes, but gets angry that Eva looks prettier than she does, so gets her fired. ❸ That is one level of inequality. She is powerful enough to get a shopgirl fired. ❹

❶ An accurate observation about a similarity

❷ This needs to address the question of inequality more directly. The terminology 'offstage character' and 'onstage' might be useful here.

❸ Accurate points, but need to connect with methods and directly contrast with what is known about Eva

❹ The question of inequality is addressed here with one clear example.

Examiner's comments

This answer would be strengthened by considering how Priestley presents inequality (that is, his methods). This would help to avoid the temptation to just retell events from the play or make unconnected observations. Even though the audience never sees Eva, they learn a lot about her. Therefore the answer could reflect examples of inequality, including families, work, and money. How Priestley explores social class is very relevant to this question. More precise references or quotations from the text with analysis explaining the effect would make this response more focused.

Sample answer 2: a strong answer

Here is an extract from a student response, with examiner's annotations and final comments. It receives high marks.

① Starts immediately with the idea of inequality

> Priestley shows the inequality of Sheila and Eva's lives by exposing the differences between them highlighted by their different social classes. ① The first image the audience has of Sheila is celebrating her engagement. The first of Eva, who is dead in the infirmary, is expressed in the Inspector's emotive language: 'Burnt her inside out'. While Sheila has been surrounded by her family, Priestley creates a lonely picture of Eva drinking disinfectant. ② Much of the inequality in their lives is down to their different social classes. Both are pretty and similar ages, but Eva doesn't have a family to support her. She is expected to work and only lowly paid jobs are available to her, which the Birlings cause her to lose. ③ Women of Sheila's social class would be expected to marry and be supported by their husbands. Sheila's father describes her as a 'lucky girl' because she has made a socially acceptable match with Gerald. Although both women had a relationship with Gerald, the outcomes are very different. ④ Gerald expresses great affection for Eva, describing her as 'pretty and warm-hearted' and 'gallant', but he would not marry a working-class girl like her. Priestley suggests that, unlike Sheila, Eva is alone, with no safety net to protect her, not even the charity which Mrs Birling could offer. ⑤

② An insightful examination of the first impressions the audience would have of the two characters.

③ Notes a significant plot point

④ A relevant point which includes context and a direct textual reference.

⑤ Several textual references which contrast the two characters

Examiner's comments

Throughout, this answer maintains its focus on the differences between the women and how hard Eva's life is in comparison to Sheila's. Priestley's methods are considered when 'emotive language' is mentioned, as well as the implicit comparisons between the two women of similar ages. A full answer might consider Sheila's growing awareness of the inequality between them.

Knowledge

Retrieval

Answer the questions below. Cover the answers column with a piece of paper and write down as many answers as you can. Check and repeat.

Questions / Answers

#	Question	Answer
1	Who are described as 'landed' people?	The Crofts
2	What social class is a factory worker?	Working class
3	What character in the play is a servant?	Edna
4	Where do Gerald and Eric socialise and meet working-class women?	The Palace Bar
5	What honour does Arthur hope will improve his social standing?	A knighthood
6	What is the metaphoric boundary the Inspector wants to break down?	The boundary between the poor working classes (like Eva) and the well-off (like the Birlings)
7	Who is described as Arthur's 'social superior'?	Sybil
8	How does Arthur describe Eric's education?	'public-school-and-varsity life'
9	What does Priestley show through the contrast between Sheila and Eva?	Social inequality – Sheila's advantages in life are contrasted with Eva's poverty
10	For what could Eva be seen as a metaphor?	The working class
11	With whom do both Eva and Sheila have a relationship?	Gerald
12	With which character is Eva particularly contrasted?	Sheila

Previous questions

Now go back and use these questions to check your knowledge of previous topics.

#	Question	Answer
1	How does the lighting change when the Inspector enters?	It becomes 'brighter and harder'
2	In which act does the Inspector deliver his warning speech to the Birlings?	Act 3

Now turn to pages 110–111 and complete Practice questions 19–21.

11 Social class and inequality

Knowledge — THEMES

12 Family and relationships

Examples of family relationships

Family life plays a central role in society and Arthur takes pride in being the head of his family. Arthur is a representative of the patriarchy. In this era, fathers would usually be responsible for supporting and protecting their wives and children. While initially presented as a happy family, who are welcoming a desirable future son-in-law, Priestley soon shows their family unit unravelling.

> **REMEMBER**
> The Birling family represents comfortable society members who are blind to the needs of others.

Husband–wife
Arthur and Sybil present a united front, fulfilling mutually expected marital roles.

Father–child
Arthur's relationship with his daughter, Sheila, is protective; he is disappointed in his son, Eric.

Mother–child
Sybil sees her children as younger and more innocent than they are; her relationships with both, particularly Eric, fracture dramatically.

Siblings
Sheila and Eric have a friendly, teasing relationship, but Sheila is aware of Eric's drinking. Later in the play, they are disappointed in their own behaviour and that of their parents.

Orphan
Both of Eva's parents are dead, so she is alone in the world and lacks the security that a supportive family could provide.

How Priestley presents family in the play

Act 1
- Setting and positioning: gathered around the dining table in their '*substantial*' home, Arthur at head of the table opposite his wife
- Stage directions: '*pleased with themselves*'
- Dialogue: 'We were having a nice family celebration tonight.'

Act 3, after the Inspector's exit
- Setting and positioning: no longer sitting together; all in different positions; Arthur is the '*only active one*'
- Stage directions: Sheila '*crying*'; Sybil '*collapsed*'
- Dialogue: Mrs Birling: 'I'm absolutely ashamed of you.'

> **REVISION TIP**
> An important structural point is that at the beginning, the Birlings are presented onstage as a united family unit, while at the end they are shown divided, particularly through the younger generation's conflict with the older generation.

Knowledge — THEMES

12 Family and relationships

Love and marriage

Sybil's views are conventional for this era. She tells Sheila that when she is married, she'll realise that men have 'important work to do'. The expectation is that Sheila's marriage to Gerald will resemble that of her parents'.

Priestley contrasts the socially acceptable engagement between Sheila and Gerald, with Gerald's hidden affair with Eva.

Quotation	Effect
'And I drink to you – and hope I can make you as happy as you deserve to be.'	In Act 1, Gerald is happily engaged to Sheila, making a public declaration of his love and commitment to Sheila.
'Yes. I suppose it was inevitable. She was young and pretty and warm-hearted – and intensely grateful.'	In Act 2, Gerald's affair with Eva is revealed. This quotation suggests that the secret affair was rooted in a genuine attraction and affection, but unequal.
'In fact, in some odd way, I rather respect you more than I've ever done before.'	In Act 2, Sheila breaks off her engagement. This quotation implies that Sheila had doubts about Gerald's previous honesty and, although she doesn't now wish to marry him, she has gained some admiration for him.

> **REMEMBER**
> Gerald is the character who provides the most affectionate portrayal of Eva. He describes her only in positive terms, but stops short of saying he loved her.

Eric and Eva's relationship

Eric is portrayed as an immature young man capable of behaving selfishly and destructively. In contrast to Gerald's affectionate relationship with Eva, Eric's is based on his drunken impulsiveness with little thought of her.

Quotation	Effect
'And I didn't even remember – that's the hellish thing.'	He sexually assaulted her when he was so drunk that he doesn't even recall the details.
'Well, I'm old enough to be married, aren't I, and I'm not married, and I hate these fat old tarts round the town'	Sex outside of marriage was strongly discouraged and could ruin a woman's reputation. Men of Eric's social class could seek the company of women outside their social class who might break with these social conventions.
'She didn't want me to marry her. Said I didn't love her'	Despite the desperation of her situation, Eva protects Eric and, once she realises the money is stolen, refuses it.

Writing about family and relationships

Sample answer 1: not a strong answer

Here is an extract from a student response, with the examiner's annotations and final comments. It receives less than half marks.

> How far does Priestley present the Birlings as a happy family?
>
> [30 marks]
> AO4 [4 marks]

① Makes accurate observations about the beginning of the play

③ Accurate observations with one textual reference, but greater analysis is needed

At the beginning of the play, the Birlings seem very happy. They are enjoying a drink and celebrating the engagement of their daughter. ① There is positively a party atmosphere going on. ② Arthur is making happy speeches and Sheila is delighted to receive her engagement ring from Gerald who Arthur says she is 'lucky' to be marrying. ③ They also have a maid who waits on them, so their lives seem very lush. Of course, they become less happy when the Inspector comes and tells them Eva is dead as that rather spoils the atmosphere. ④

② Overly informal expression of ideas without providing any direct textual reference to support

④ Notes a turning point but doesn't analyse it

Examiner's comments

While accurately noting that the Birlings largely seem happy at the beginning of the play, small hints that all might not be well are not mentioned in this answer. At times, the choice of vocabulary is very casual: 'party atmosphere', 'lush'. Greater use of methods and literary terminology could be included, such as 'dialogue', 'stage directions', and 'turning point'. Insight into the false assumptions that are the basis for the Birlings' happiness, such as that capitalism will only benefit society or that their actions aren't harmful to others, would also improve this answer.

LINK

To revise the presentation of the Birlings, see Plot on pages 2–19. For more about Methods, see pages 20–27.

REVISION TIP

List the writer's methods covered in this book and list at least one example of each.

Knowledge 71

Knowledge — THEMES

12 Family and relationships

Sample answer 2: a strong answer

Here is an extract from a student response, with examiner's annotations and final comments. It receives high marks.

> At the beginning of Act 1, the Birlings are largely presented as a happy family. In the opening stage directions, Priestley describes them as 'celebrating' and 'very pleased with themselves'. ❶ Given Sheila's engagement their celebratory mood is understandable, but Priestley foreshadows that all may not be well. Despite her happiness, Sheila speaks in a 'half serious, half playful' way about Gerald having ignored her for a long period and warns him to 'be careful'. ❷ Eric, who in the stage directions is said to be 'not quite at ease', has been drinking heavily and his interruptions, such as his sudden 'guffaws' seem to annoy his parents. ❸ Priestley's use of irony also suggests future unhappiness. The audience are aware that Arthur's predictions about the Titanic and war are entirely wrong as are his confidence that capitalism will necessarily lead to progress and peace. ❹ However, the overriding impression of the opening is of high-spirits and that it is likely that more happiness awaits this family. With the inciting incident of the arrival of the Inspector, the dynamics of the family gathering change entirely. One by one, the faults of the family are revealed, demonstrating the dark secrets that lie beneath this outwardly happy family. ❺

❶ Direct textual reference in response to question and use of terminology

❷ A nuanced discussion of foreshadowing hinting at problems in Gerald and Sheila's relationship

❸ Some insight into Eric's possible unhappiness but this could be analysed further

❹ Identifies Priestley's uses of irony to make a point about the superficial aspect of Arthur's happiness

❺ Shows an understanding of the play's structure and responds to the extent of the family's happiness

Examiner's comments

This response confidently weaves in a discussion of the playwright's methods (foreshadowing, irony, inciting incident) while remaining focused on answering the question. A full answer could consider the way different members of the family react to the Inspector's revelations and what that reveals about their characters. A discussion of the dramatic importance of showing a family whose fortunes change throughout the play would also be appropriate.

Retrieval

Answer the questions below. Cover the answers column with a piece of paper and write down as many answers as you can. Check and repeat.

Questions | Answers

#	Question	Answer
1	In this play, which family member is shown as responsible for financially supporting their family?	The father/Arthur Birling
2	How is Arthur representative of the patriarchy?	As the father of the family, he thinks he is responsible for supporting and protecting his family
3	Why does Eva need to get a job?	She is an orphan with no one to support her
4	How is it shown that Gerald's relationship with Sheila is more socially acceptable than his relationship with Eva?	He makes a public declaration of his engagement with Sheila while keeping secret his relationship with Eva, who he will not marry
5	In the stage directions, the Birlings are described as '*pleased with* _____'?	'*pleased with themselves*'
6	What is the turning point in Priestley's presentation of the Birlings as a happy family?	The Inspector's entrance
7	How is Sybil described after the Inspector's exit?	'*collapsed*'
8	Who says, 'She didn't want me to marry her.'?	Eric
9	What technique is used when Sheila talks about Gerald having ignored her?	Foreshadowing
10	Who makes a 'half serious, half playful' warning to Gerald?	Sheila

Previous questions

Now go back and use these questions to check your knowledge of previous topics.

Questions | Answers

#	Question	Answer
1	Why does Eric say he didn't confide in his father?	He is 'not the kind of father a chap could go to when he's in trouble'
2	For what could Eva be seen as a metaphor?	The working class

> Now turn to pages 106–107 and complete Practice questions 11–14.

Knowledge — THEMES

13 Money

Examples of money in the play

Priestley mentions money explicitly and implicitly throughout the play. Business is rarely far from Arthur's mind – he even mentions it during his toast. Money is shown to be important, for status and comfort, but also for survival.

Business
Act 1: 'working together – for lower costs and higher prices.'

Wages
Act 1: 'They wanted the rates raised so that they could average about twenty-five shillings a week.'

Rent
Act 2: 'she hadn't a penny and was going to be turned out of the miserable back room she had.'

Gifts
Act 2: 'I insisted on a parting gift of enough money […] to see her through to the end of the year.'

Stolen money
Act 3: 'The girl discovered that this money you were giving her was stolen, didn't she?'

Socialism versus capitalism

Socialism

Arthur: 'He was prejudiced from the start. Probably a Socialist or some sort of crank.'

The Inspector represents socialism. When Priestley wrote the play, there was interest in increasing social benefits and a strengthening of unions. The Inspector thinks it's better to 'ask for the earth than to take it', contrasting the workers asking for a raise with the manufacturers taking more than their fair share.

Capitalism

Arthur: 'you'll be living in a world that'll have forgotten all these Capital versus Labour agitations […] There'll be peace and prosperity and rapid progress everywhere'.

Arthur represents capitalism, which he believes will lead to progress, symbolised by the *Titanic* and automobiles. He bases his opinions on his own experience and the success of his business. However, without social benefits, people like Eva must rely on private charities, which in her case failed her.

Manufacturers versus workers

Although manufacturing was booming at this time, workers were often poorly paid. This led to a period of strikes amongst the workforce. Priestley reflects an aspect of this unrest in Act 1, when Eva's attempt to lead a strike action in Birling's factory was unsuccessful.

Quotation	Effect
'there's a lot of wild talk about possible labour trouble'	Arthur dismisses the concerns of the workers and shows a lack of sympathy for their hard lives.
'they could go and work somewhere else'	Arthur knows that it would not be easy for the fired workers to get new jobs.
'Pitiful affair.'	The workers held out for two months, but this phrase suggests they were in a poor state, weak, hungry, and defeated, when they returned.
'But these girls aren't cheap labour – they're *people*.'	Unlike her father, Sheila sees the humanity of the workers.

> **REMEMBER**
>
> You will not be expected to include external historic details in your answer. You only need to show an understanding of the ideas Priestley is conveying within the world of the play.

Depictions of people living in poverty

Eva is used as an example of what can happen when a person has no family, community, or government support.

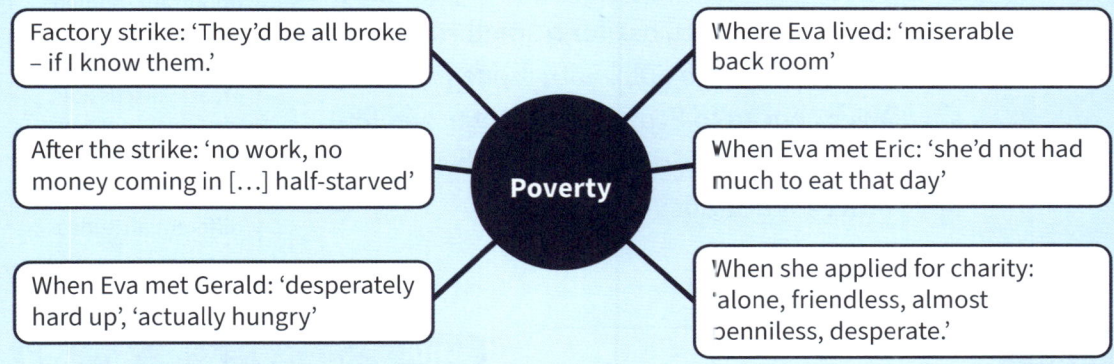

- Factory strike: 'They'd be all broke – if I know them.'
- After the strike: 'no work, no money coming in [...] half-starved'
- When Eva met Gerald: 'desperately hard up', 'actually hungry'
- Where Eva lived: 'miserable back room'
- When Eva met Eric: 'she'd not had much to eat that day'
- When she applied for charity: 'alone, friendless, almost penniless, desperate.'

Money as a metaphor

> 'You made her pay a heavy price for that. And now she'll make you pay a heavier price still.'

Although money is discussed explicitly, it is also used as a metaphor, for example:

- when the Inspector refers to the emotional and reputational 'price' the Birlings will have to pay for what they have done
- in the 'heavy price', ultimately her life, that Eva had to pay for daring to ask for a pay rise.

Knowledge

Knowledge THEMES

13 Money

Writing about money

Sample answer 1: not a strong answer

Here is an extract from a student response, with the examiner's annotations and final comments. It receives less than half marks.

> How does Priestley present the characters' different attitudes towards money?
> **[30 marks]**
> **AO4 [4 marks]**

❶ Shows some understanding but could mention 'attitudes' in this opening

❷ Locates an early reference to money but needs more analysis

❸ Locates another important moment which would benefit from greater discussion

❹ Identifies different attitudes

> Money is an important theme in the play because Eva dies because she is poor. This is particularly shocking because the wealthy characters in the play could have saved her, if they wanted to. ❶ We know that money is important to Arthur because he speaks about it from the opening of the play and his desire to improve his business by working with the Crofts. ❷ But he is so focused on having money for himself and his family, he doesn't think about his workers, willing to watch them suffer when they ask for a small raise. ❸ The main time we see Sybil with money is when she denies charity to Eva. The Inspector and Eric both think Sybil was wrong, so they obviously have different attitudes to money. ❹

Examiner's comments

This extract notes some instances where money is important, such as Arthur's reaction to the strike and Sybil's withholding of the charity money. However, the characters' attitudes and the reason for them could be developed further. A more detailed analysis of Priestley's methods, such as his use of contrast between the Birlings and Eva or the emotive language used by the Inspector to show how poverty affects Eva, would show a wider range of skills. The contrasting beliefs of the Inspector and Arthur about workers' pay could also be explored.

LINK
Money can be linked to the theme of social class and inequality (see pages 64–67).

REVISION TIP
Go through this answer and make notes on textual references and methods that could be included. Then rewrite it with that additional information.

Sample answer 2: a strong answer

Here is an extract from a student response, with examiner's annotations and final comments. It receives high marks.

> One of the differences in attitudes towards money is shown by Priestley's presentation of the characters who have money, represented by the Birlings and Gerald, and those who do not, represented by Eva. While the wealthy characters are seen celebrating and enjoying champagne, Priestley presents a dismal portrait of Eva's life: '…alone, friendless, almost penniless, desperate'. ❶ The play is set in 1912 when the inequality of wealth was felt very strongly. ❷ At the play's opening, the Birlings have enjoyed a large meal, whereas Priestley mentions more than once that Eva is hungry. ❸ Arthur feels that his wealth is down to his hard work and experience, but Priestley shows that Eva's poverty is not due to her carelessness as she is described as a 'good worker'. However, despite her best efforts she finds herself penniless. Gerald says she 'lived very economically' on the money he gave her, money that he apparently could easily spare. ❹ Another key contrast is between the Inspector, who promotes Priestley's socialist point of view, while Arthur represents capitalism. Writing the play after the Second World War when many were thinking of creating a new and better world, Priestley uses the character of the Inspector to warn of the dangers of capitalism which does not take into account the 'millions' of people whose lives are intertwined with theirs. ❺

❶ A clear statement of differences with well-chosen examples from the play

❷ A concise, relevant contextual point

❸ A contrast between characters

❹ Well-chosen quotations to show Eva's attitude towards money

❺ Begins to explore Priestley's intentions within the context of post-First World War period

Examiner's comments

This answer looks at characters' different attitudes from two perspectives, whether or not they have money and whether they believe in capitalism or socialism. A full answer could explore Sheila's developing attitudes to those with less money.

Knowledge

Retrieval

Answer the questions below. Cover the answers column with a piece of paper and write down as many answers as you can. Check and repeat.

Questions | Answers

#	Question	Answer
1	Who gave Eva a parting gift of money?	Gerald
2	What wages did the factory workers strike for?	25 shillings a week
3	Who stole money?	Eric
4	Who represents a socialist point of view?	The Inspector
5	What economic point of view does Arthur represent?	Capitalist
6	What are two signs of progress that Arthur mentions?	The *Titanic*; automobiles
7	What does Arthur mentioning business during his toast show?	That money is rarely far from his mind, even during a family celebration
8	What did Arthur say the workers could do if they didn't like the wages?	Go and work somewhere else
9	Sheila says the workers are not just 'cheap _____'?	'cheap labour'
10	What literary technique is used when the Inspector says that the Birlings will 'pay a heavier price still'?	Metaphor
11	What does Sybil deny Eva?	Charity money
12	Which character in the play is an example of what can happen when a person has no family, community, or government support?	Eva

Previous questions

Now go back and use these questions to check your knowledge of previous topics.

Questions | Answers

#	Question	Answer
1	The Birlings' home could be seen as a microcosm of what?	Late Edwardian society
2	Who says, 'She didn't want me to marry her.'?	Eric

> Now turn to page 109 and complete Practice question 17.

Knowledge — THEMES — 14

14 Responsibility and guilt

Responsibility – key quotations

A key message of the play is the responsibility that people owe to one another. Priestley reveals how the Birlings' and Gerald's self-interest and lack of empathy are harmful. Some examples of their different senses of responsibility towards Eva are shown below.

Arthur	Sybil
'Still, I can't accept any responsibility. If we were all responsible for everything that happened to everybody we'd had anything to do with, it would be very awkward, wouldn't it?'	'I'm sorry she should have come to such a horrible end. But I accept no blame for it at all.'
Gerald	**Sheila**
'She didn't blame me at all. I wish to God she had now.'	'It's the only time I've ever done anything like that, and I'll never, never do it again to anybody.'
Eric	**Inspector**
'I was in a hell of a state about it.'	'You'll be able to divide the responsibility between you when I've gone.'

Attitudes about responsibility

Arthur

In Act 1, the Inspector first enters shortly after Arthur explains his philosophy of 'a man has to mind his own business and look after himself and his own'. Arthur's experience as a hard-headed businessman influences his attitude: he denies responsibility for Eva's death, saying that he fired her two years ago and that it was a sound business decision. In Act 3, his attitude wavers when he learns of Eric's involvement. However, when he suspects it is all a hoax, he feels relieved of all responsibility.

Sheila

In Act 1, Sheila's sympathetic nature appears in her initial reaction to Eva's death. When she learns of her share of the responsibility, she immediately admits to it and is shaken by the effect of her impulsive actions. In Act 3, she continues to reflect on the Inspector's message. She shows the greatest sense of responsibility of them all.

Sybil

On a superficial level, Sybil would seem to have a sense of social responsibility because of her charity work. However, it becomes clear that she doesn't use this truly for the good of the needy and instead wields her power to deprive Eva of help. She is perhaps the most steadfast in denying any responsibility or a need for atonement.

> **REVISION TIP**
> Priestley shows varying degrees of responsibility between the characters, so make sure you understand their differences.

Knowledge — THEMES

14 Responsibility and guilt

Social versus personal responsibility

Social responsibility

The Inspector is arguing that people should have a greater sense of responsibility, not just to those personally known to them, but to all who are vulnerable. This is social responsibility. In his final speech, he makes clear there is not just one Eva Smith but 'millions and millions' of others whose 'suffering and chance of happiness' is 'intertwined with our lives'. This is linked to Priestley's belief in socialism. The Inspector asserts that 'Public men […] have responsibilities as well as privileges'.

Personal responsibility

Gerald acknowledges a degree of personal responsibility for his relationship with Eva and wishes that she had blamed him more. He also feels guilty for how he treated Sheila during this time. However, unlike Sheila, whose attitudes towards social responsibility have changed, Gerald never indicates that the current social order is in any way to blame for Eva's sad end. Once he believes it is a hoax, he reverts to his previous confidence about his life and the way that society is organised.

Methods used to explore guilt

Methods used to explore guilt

- **Repetition**: Sheila: 'I'll never, never do it again to anybody.'
  This emphasis shows how strongly she feels.

- **Rhetorical questions**: Sheila: 'How could I know what would happen afterwards?'
  She is trying to ease her guilt.

- **Irregular punctuation**: Gerald: 'In that case – as I'm rather more – upset – '
  His fragmented lines show his strong emotions.

- **Structure**: the time loop effect
  This suggests the Birlings may have to hear the Inspector's message repeatedly until they accept their guilt.

- **Stage directions**: '*Eric enters, looking extremely pale and distressed.*'
  His altered appearance indicates his emotional response.

- **Silence**: both Gerald and Eric do not 'reply' when asked probing questions
  Their lack of response is an admission of guilt.

- **Conflict**: Birling: 'You're the one I blame for this.'
  Arthur lashes out at Eric to deflect blame from himself.

- **Emotional expression**: Sheila '*crying quietly*'
  This suggests the deep grief she feels at her guilt.

> **REVISION TIP**
> Note the methods above, then go through the play trying to find other examples of each method.

Key terms — Make sure you can write a definition for this key term: rhetorical question

14

Writing about responsibility and guilt

Sample answer 1: not a strong answer

Here is an extract from a student response, with the examiner's annotations and final comments. It receives less than half marks.

> How does Priestley explore the idea of responsibility through the characters?
> **[30 marks]**
> **AO4 [4 marks]**

> The Birlings have different reactions to the news of Eva Smith's death. It is told to them by the Inspector in a shocking way but, at first, they have no idea what it has to do with them. ❶ Arthur believes only in being responsible for himself and lets everyone know this. However, the Inspector keeps giving more details, until Arthur finally admits he fired Eva. But still, he doesn't really accept responsibility. He just thinks it was a good business decision. ❷ This really annoys the Inspector who by the end is shouting at the Birlings to listen to him. I think he does this because he has socialist points of view and wants the Birlings to accept them. ❸ If they had taken more care, Eva would still be alive. I think that Eric should take more of the blame as his behaviour was particularly heartless. His father seems angrier about him stealing the money from the firm than anything else. In the end, Priestley seems to be saying it is on your conscience if you treat people badly. ❹

❶ Although true, this doesn't directly address the question.

❷ Shows understanding of the plot, but needs to explore 'how' Priestley presents this – through dialogue, stage directions, etc

❸ This is informally expressed and would benefit from more direct reference to the text.

❹ Expresses a personal response, but needs to connect more directly to the question and the idea of responsibility

Examiner's comments

Although an understanding of the plot is shown, there is no examination of methods. Instead, there is an inclination to simply retell incidents. A stronger approach might have been to contrast different characters' reactions and to look more deeply at the different types of responsibility that Priestley is writing about.

REVISION TIP
Make a bullet point plan for how you would answer this question.

LINK
To compare the different characters look at Characters on pages 28–63.

Knowledge 81

Knowledge — THEMES

14 Responsibility and guilt

Sample answer 2: a strong answer

Here is an extract from a student response, with examiner's annotations and final comments. It receives high marks.

> Priestley shows the importance of a sense of personal and social responsibility explicitly in the third act. After uncovering the responsibility that each of the Birlings and Gerald Croft bear for Eva Smith's tragic ending, the Inspector states the moral of the play: 'We are responsible for each other'. ❶ This suggests more than just personal responsibility but also a greater social responsibility for the vulnerable, as represented by Eva Smith. However, the dialogue that follows the Inspector's exit makes clear that this is not an easy lesson to accept. For example, Arthur says to Eric, 'You're the one I blame for this'. This suggests that Arthur doesn't accept his role in Eva's downfall. ❷ Arthur's unwillingness to learn the Inspector's lesson is shown by the mood change when they believe it was all a hoax, with Arthur raising a toast to them all. This suggests at least a partial return to the ease seen early in Act One, as they resume their previous self-interested ways. ❸ However, unlike her parents, Sheila has changed. She accuses the others of 'pretending everything's just as it was before'. Eric too seems altered, though in a less defined way. It is ironic that Arthur utters the words, 'can't even take a joke', only for the final telephone call to make clear that this was not a joke. ❹

❶ Identifies the Inspector as the moral messenger promoting social responsibility

❷ Provides evidence and shows an understanding of the play

❸ Notes mood changes, physical actions, and makes connections between different scenes

❹ Understands Priestley's use of irony, with a character saying the opposite of what is true

Examiner's comments

This answer considers a number of writer's methods, such as mood changes, irony, dialogue, and structure. Different ideas regarding responsibility are examined, particularly through the presentation of Sheila and Arthur.

A full answer might consider the chain of responsibility between the characters and the reason why social responsibility is particularly important given the play's context.

Retrieval

Answer the questions below. Cover the answers column with a piece of paper and write down as many answers as you can. Check and repeat.

Questions | Answers

#	Question	Answer
1	What method is used when Sheila says 'never, never'?	Repetition
2	Who enters shortly after Arthur talks about the responsibility of looking after oneself?	The Inspector
3	In which act does Arthur learn of Eric's involvement with Eva?	Act 3
4	What are two examples of different types of responsibility explored in the play?	Personal and social responsibility
5	Who argues for greater social responsibility?	The Inspector
6	Complete the quotation: 'You'll be able to divide the _____ between you when I've gone.'	'You'll be able to divide the responsibility between you when I've gone.'
7	Whose lines become fragmented when he is distressed?	Gerald
8	Does Gerald demonstrate personal responsibility or social responsibility, and how is this shown?	Personal responsibility – he feels personally responsible for Eva, but does not connect this with a need for society to change
9	What belief of Priestley's is the Inspector expressing when he says: 'Public men […] have responsibilities as well as privileges.'?	Social responsibility
10	Which character is perhaps the most steadfast in denying any responsibility or a need for atonement?	Sybil
11	What is the effect of the time loop structure on the message about the Birlings' responsibility?	The characters may have to hear the message repeatedly until they accept their guilt

Previous questions

Now go back and use these questions to check your knowledge of previous topics.

Questions | Answers

#	Question	Answer
1	Who are described as 'landed' people?	The Crofts
2	Who represents a socialist point of view?	The Inspector

Now turn to pages 111–112 and complete Practice questions 22–23.

Knowledge THEMES

15 Gender roles

Gender roles in Edwardian England

In Edwardian England, women were denied many rights and opportunities. For example, women did not have the right to vote and many jobs were not available to them. Women who were pregnant and unmarried would be subjected to discrimination, which is likely why Eva lied and gave the name 'Mrs Birling' when she sought charity. Men were generally expected to provide for and protect their female family members.

Priestley often wrote sympathetically of women's lives and this can be seen in his empathetic presentation of the characters of Eva and Sheila.

> **REMEMBER**
> 'Roles' in this sense, means positions in society, such as functions within a family, organisation, or community, and the 'gender roles' discussed are those typically assumed by men or women at the time the play was set.

How women are presented

Presentation of women in the play

- **Charity:** Sybil undertakes charity work, but the organisation makes judgements about which women are worthy of their aid.

- **Work:** The upper-class female characters don't undertake paid work outside the home, while the working-class women have jobs. Eva works in a factory and a shop and Edna works as a maid. These are the sorts of jobs that would be most easily available to them, though it is stressed that Eva was 'lucky' to get the job at Milwards, probably because it was a more sophisticated job than her previous employment.

- **Society's norms:** Gerald and Eric euphemistically refer to the sex workers who work at the Palace Theatre Bar, '[…] a favourite haunt of the women of the town.' Priestley suggests that the women at the Palace Bar were behaving outside society's norms. It is implied that women there might exchange anything from a flirtation to sex for some financial help.

- **Marriage:** Sybil says 'When you're married you'll realize that men with important work to do sometimes have to spend nearly all their time and energy on their business.'

- **Fashion and beauty:** Sheila spends time and money on clothes and feels envious of Eva's looks, saying 'But she was very pretty and looked as if she could take care of herself.'

How men are presented

- Responsible for looking after self and family: Arthur states this philosophy in Act 1
- Expected to be interested in current affairs: Arthur lectures the others on progress, politics, and economics
- The Inspector seeks to bring about justice: he aims to shame and educate the Birlings and Gerald for the greater good
- Allowed to enjoy leisure: Arthur plays golf, while Eric and Gerald are young men about town, seeking female company
- Their role is to earn money: Arthur and Gerald are both businessmen

Men's attitudes to women

The way Priestley presents the men in the play often suggests that they believe women to be weaker or less important.

Attitude	Evidence
Condescending	Arthur: 'Yes, but you've got to remember, my boy, that clothes mean something quite different to a woman […] a […] token of their self-respect.'
Protective	Gerald: 'I think Miss Birling ought to be excused any more of this questioning.'
Disrespectful	Eric: 'I hate those fat old tarts round the town'

Importance of beauty

Though Eva is an offstage character, Priestley emphasises her attractiveness, something which every character except for Sybil mentions. Upon learning of Eva's death, Sheila's first two questions are about her age and if she was pretty. Eva's prettiness contributes to her entanglements with the Birlings and adds another layer of poignancy to her death.

'she was very pretty and looked as if she could take care of herself'	'She wasn't pretty when I saw her today, but she had been pretty – very pretty'	'she was pretty and a good sport'
Sheila's jealousy of Eva's prettiness led her to make a complaint against her, and she assumed that she wouldn't be badly affected by being fired. This shows Sheila's superficial concerns and her ignorance of the difficulties of a shop assistant's life.	The Inspector, in his possibly sarcastic reply, is reminding Sheila of Eva's ugly death from poisoning and contrasting it with her beauty when alive. This adds to the poignancy of her death.	Eric chooses Eva over the 'fat old tarts' at the Palace Bar because she is young, pretty, and apparently available, but then treats her, as the Inspector says, 'as if she was an animal'. In this case, her attractiveness has made her a target.

Knowledge — THEMES

15 Gender roles

Writing about gender roles

Sample answer 1: not a strong answer

Here is an extract from a student response, with the examiner's annotations and final comments. It receives less than half marks.

> How does Priestley present women and their concerns in the play?
> [30 marks]
> AO4 [4 marks]

❶ This isn't entirely correct. Although Edna is a small role, she is one of three onstage female characters. Eva, though an offstage character, could also be discussed.

❸ This is an accurate textual reference, but again, more meaning could be drawn from it.

❹ This lacks insight. Although Sybil serves on a committee, there isn't evidence that she cares about people.

> There are two women in the play and Priestley shows them to be mainly interested in fashion and marriage. The two women are Sybil, the mother of the family, and her daughter, Sheila. ❶ When they are first presented to the audience they are celebrating Sheila's engagement. This shows that marriage is important to them and the engagement ring is an important prop in the play. It symbolises the love between Gerald and Sheila. Sheila expects to become a wife like her mother. ❷ Sheila is very concerned with appearances. She seems obsessed with Eva being pretty and Eric says she is 'potty' about fashions. ❸ I think this shows that she has a very limited life. Her mother doesn't say that much in Act 1, but in Act 2, we learn that she is on a charity committee so that means that she must care at least a bit about other people. ❹ Women couldn't vote. ❺ It is hard to say how he feels about the women in this play overall, as they aren't entirely sympathetic. ❻

❷ This is correct, and useful to spot the importance of the ring and what it symbolises, but the point could be developed further with more evidence of her attitude towards marriage.

❺ This is true, but a bolted-on fact like this without connection to the question will not be rewarded.

❻ This is an underdeveloped point, without direct support from the text. Arguably, Sheila is the most sympathetic onstage character in the play.

Examiner's comments

Although this answer displays a recall of some events in the play and attempts to note some methods, such as the use of a prop, symbolism, and one direct textual refence, it doesn't offer enough insight. Some points are offered without support and the differences between Sybil and Sheila aren't considered. Sybil, in particular, requires more understanding. For example, Priestley doesn't show her being charitable and she may serve on the committee for social or status reasons.

LINK

For more insight into Sybil's behaviour, see Plot Act 2, and the characters of Sybil and Sheila on pages 10–11, and Characters on pages 34–45.

Sample answer 2: a strong answer

Here is an extract from a student response, with examiner's annotations and final comments. It receives high marks.

1 Begins with an accurate contextual point related to Priestley's presentation of women

2 Explores author's methods, such as offstage characters and use of a catalyst

4 Well-expressed detail which reflects on both Sybil and Eva's roles

> Priestley presents the roles and expectations of upper middle-class women in Edwardian England to be very different from working-class women. Sheila and her mother are shown to be in a secure home without the necessity to work outside it, whereas Edna, the third onstage female character, is a maid shown waiting on the family. This gives a sense of how the comfort of some women is at the expense of others. **1** Another example of this is when Sheila, as a valued customer, is able to get Eva, a shopgirl, fired. Eva, though an offstage character, has a huge presence in the play, as the announcement of her death is the catalyst for the play's actions and each character describes their interactions with her. **2** She represents the concerns and hardships that could face working-class women: insecure jobs, unwanted sexual advances and unplanned single motherhood. **3** It is ironic that when she approaches Sybil's charity, particularly established for women in distress like her, she is turned away by her. **4** However, the portrayal of Sheila is less negative than her mother. Although Sheila is initially presented as a character concerned with superficial prettiness and fashion, as the play progresses, Priestley uses stage directions to heighten the impression of her deep and sincere emotions: 'crying silently' and 'distressed'. **5**

3 Concisely considers Eva's gender-based hardships

5 Accurately cites stage directions to support a point about Sheila

Examiner's comments

In this answer, a number of important points are made concisely. In a longer answer, Eva and Sheila's relationship with Gerald could perhaps be discussed.

REVISION TIP

When revising the character of Sheila, note the stage directions that Priestley uses to show how affected she is by the events of the evening.

Retrieval

Answer the questions below. Cover the answers column with a piece of paper and write down as many answers as you can. Check and repeat.

Questions / Answers

#	Question	Answer
1	Could women vote in 1912 (when the play is set)?	No
2	Why did Eva give the name 'Mrs Birling' when she sought help from the charity?	Because, being pregnant and unmarried, she would have been discriminated against
3	Where did Eva work after leaving her job at the Birlings' factory?	Milwards
4	What did Sybil say Sheila would realise when she was married?	That men sometimes had important work to do that took up their time
5	How is work different for the upper- or middle-class and working-class women in the play?	The upper- and middle-class women in the play do not undertake paid work outside the home, the working-class women do
6	Who said Eva looked like, 'she could take care of herself'?	Sheila
7	How does Priestley use irony in presenting Sybil's charity work?	The charity is meant to help women in distress but doesn't help Eva
8	Which important woman in the play is an offstage character?	Eva
9	What were the first two questions Sheila asked about Eva?	Her age and if she was pretty
10	What is the effect of the Inspector's description of Eva: 'She wasn't pretty when I saw her today, but she had been pretty – very pretty.'?	It reminds Sheila of Eva's ugly death from poisoning and contrasts it with her beauty when alive, adding to the poignancy of her death
11	The Inspector says Eric treated Eva like what?	'an animal'

Previous questions

Now go back and use these questions to check your knowledge of previous topics.

#	Question	Answer
1	Why is Gerald considered a desirable match for Sheila?	He comes from a wealthy family
2	What technique is used when Sheila talks about Gerald having ignored her?	Foreshadowing

Now turn to pages 109–110 and complete Practice questions 18–19.

15 Gender roles

Knowledge — THEMES — 16

16 Generations

Differences between the generations

Priestley contrasts the concerns of the younger generation with those of the older.

- Sybil is surprised at the impression the Inspector has on Sheila, to which the Inspector replies: 'We often do on the young ones. They're more impressionable.'

- Arthur's attitude towards Eric's behaviour: Arthur shows a lack of respect for Eric who he says is 'spoilt' and who he blames for the potential scandal.

- Sybil's attitude towards social conventions: Sybil believes in observing social niceties, scolding others for inappropriate dinner table talk and use of slang. She takes offence at the Inspector's manner.

- Sybil and Sheila's reaction to the Inspector: Sheila is respectful to, and fearful of, the Inspector, whereas Sybil thinks she has the upper hand.

- Sybil and Sheila's attitudes towards working-class women: Sybil dismisses Eva due to her impertinence given her working-class status, but Sheila argues against building walls between people.

- The younger Birlings and older Birlings' reactions after thinking it was all a hoax: Arthur and Sybil are relieved and celebrate, while Sheila and Eric continue to be unsettled by what they have learned.

REMEMBER
Although not members of the Birling family, the Inspector is closer in age to the older generation and Gerald is closer to the younger.

REVISION TIP
Make a chart showing the differences between the younger and older characters.

Presentation of different generations

Younger Birlings
The younger Birlings have benefited from the comfort of their parents' wealth. Eric has been privately educated and Sheila enjoys the fashions of the day. He is a careless young man about town, while she has made a suitable marriage match. However, after the revelations of the evening, they have changed from their previous complacency.

Older Birlings
The older Birlings are enjoying their upper middle-class lives at a time when manufacturing could bring great wealth. Arthur credits his success to hard work as a young man when he was 'short of cash' but also had 'a bit of fun'. Arthur views the prosperity, progress, and relative peace of this era as continuing on into the future.

REVISION TIP
Although the Edwardian age was often seen as a 'gilded age', Priestley, in hindsight, suggests that the older generation was blind to the destruction to come, including the First World War.

Knowledge — THEMES

16 Generations

Conflict between the generations

Example	Method	Analysis
Arthur versus Eric 'Unless you brighten your ideas, you'll never be in a position to let anybody stay or to tell anybody to go.'	Ridicule, denigration	Arthur shows how little he respects Eric, who he believes has had an easy life and has not shone at work.
Sybil versus Sheila 'Please don't contradict me like that.'	Assumes high status; emphasises her social skills in adversity	Sybil speaks as strongly as she can while maintaining a polite ('Please') demeanour. She assumes Sheila should defer to her.
Sheila versus Sybil 'Mother – stop – stop!'	Interruption and repetition	Sheila repeatedly tries to stop her mother, who is taking the wrong approach with the Inspector and making matters worse.
Eric versus Sybil '(almost threatening her) You don't understand anything.'	Stage directions	From the **subtext** of minor conflict, the potential threat of physical violence has exploded.

Arthur's attitude towards the young generation

- Advises: 'I say, you can ignore all this silly pessimistic talk.'
- Praises: 'You're just the kind of son-in-law I always wanted.'
- Scolds: 'Are you listening, Sheila? This concerns you too.'
- Protects: 'there isn't the slightest reason why my daughter should be dragged into this unpleasant business.'

REMEMBER
Eric's attitude to Arthur is particularly distant. He says Arthur is not 'the kind of father a chap could go to when he's in trouble'.

Use of irony

Throughout the play, Priestley uses irony to show how wrong Arthur's advice and predictions to the younger generation are. Particularly significant is that the play takes place two years before the First World War, so the audience would be aware that Arthur's advice that they are 'marrying at a very good time' and that the talk of war is 'nonsense' is wrong. Priestley repeatedly sets Arthur up to have his hopes for the future dashed, from his daughter's advantageous marriage to his knighthood.

Key terms — Make sure you can write a definition for this key term: subtext

16

Writing about generations

Sample answer 1: not a strong answer

Here is an extract from a student response, with the examiner's annotations and final comments. It receives less than half marks.

> How far does Priestley present Sybil and Sheila as contrasting characters?
> **[30 marks]**
> **AO4 [4 marks]**

1 Starts with an appropriate contrast and one textual reference

2 Other comparisons are made, but they aren't related to the Inspector or Eva Smith

3 This speculation needs to be connected more precisely to the text.

4 This ends with a very general observation, which lacks insight.

> Sheila is much more frightened of the Inspector, whereas Sybil is 'cold' and haughty. **1** It is interesting that although they are very different, Priestley has given them similar sounding names, both starting with 'S' and are two syllables long. They are also both middle class and interested in clothes, but Sheila is generally less formal and more emotional. **2** Sybil just wants to get rid of the Inspector. However, he is stubborn and she ends up saying much more than she should. I think if Sheila had been on the charitable committee she would have given Eva the money because she is generally more soft-hearted. **3** Generally the Inspector is able to bully Sheila more than he can Sybil, something that Sybil is proud of. Priestley shows the characters have similarities and differences. **4**

Examiner's comments

This answer would have benefited from a few minutes' planning as it currently jumps from observation to observation without clear linking ideas or providing support from the text. Beyond the speculation about their names, which is not relevant, Priestley's methods are not considered.

LINK

For more information on Sheila and Sybil and their contrasting reactions to the Inspector, see Plot, Act 2, pages 10–11, and Characters on pages 34–45.

REVISION TIP
Make a detailed plan for how you would answer this question, noting textual references and methods.

REVISION TIP
Make a chart comparing the stage directions Priestley uses to describe Sybil and Sheila's actions and attitudes.

Knowledge

Knowledge THEMES

16 Generations

Sample answer 2: a strong answer

Here is an extract from a student response, with examiner's annotations and final comments. It receives high marks.

> Sybil and Sheila are presented as very different people. Sheila is sensitive and open to the Inspector's message of greater empathy and social responsibility. She quickly accepts that she injured Eva by getting her fired. Sibyl's sense of social superiority leaves her unable to grasp the Inspector's message, and her prejudices, based on social class, led her to deny Eva vital charity. ❶ Priestley ends Act 2 with Sheila's anguished cry that she had 'begged' her mother to stop, highlighting their contrasting natures and responses. Priestley uses Sheila and Sybil to represent different generations' approach to social inequality. Sybil stubbornly refuses to accept responsibility while Sheila is shown to be changed by the end of the play. This confirms the Inspector's observation that the younger generation are often more open to his message. ❷ Priestley's use of stage directions also highlights their differences, with Sheila's 'half-stifled sob', when she realises the wrong she did Eva, contrasting with Sibyl speaking 'rather grandly' to the Inspector. Priestley portrays Sheila as highly emotional, but Sybil only becomes truly agitated when she realises Eric's involvement and the implications for the family. ❸

❶ Identifies contrasts in the characters' reactions to the Inspector's message

❷ Identifies the theme of social responsibility and the differences between the characters

❸ Uses textual references from the stage directions to show methods Priestley uses to show their contrasting natures

Examiner's comments

This response provides an insightful reading of Sheila and Sybil's relationship with many appropriate textual references, and considers how they are representative of different generations. It analyses some of Priestley's methods, particularly stage directions, and develops an interpretation of Sheila's emotional nature.

Retrieval

Answer the questions below. Cover the answers column with a piece of paper and write down as many answers as you can. Check and repeat.

Questions / Answers

#	Question	Answer
1	How does Priestley convey Sybil's sense of social superiority?	He shows her correcting the behaviour of her children and Arthur, taking offence at the Inspector's manner, and judging Eva on the basis of her social class
2	Which generation celebrates when they think the Inspector's visit was a hoax?	The older generation
3	How is the difference between Sybil and Sheila's attitudes to working-class women shown?	Sybil dismisses Eva due to her impertinence given her working-class status, but Sheila argues against building walls between people
4	Who repeatedly tries to interrupt Sybil?	Sheila
5	Who almost threatens Sybil?	Eric
6	Who complains about 'pessimistic talk'?	Arthur
7	What method is used when Arthur wrongly predicts future peace?	Irony
8	'Unless you brighten your ideas, you'll never be in a position to let anybody stay or to tell anybody to go.' What does this quotation show about how Arthur feels about Eric?	It shows how little Arthur respects Eric, who he believes has had an easy life and has not worked hard
9	How does Sybil enter in Act 2?	'briskly and self-confidently'
10	Which generation is more open to the Inspector's ideas?	The younger generation
11	What is the effect of their greater openness to the Inspector's message?	It suggests that the younger generation are more likely to change the future

Previous questions

Now go back and use these questions to check your knowledge of previous topics.

#	Question	Answer
1	Who does Eric blame for killing his child?	His mother
2	Why did Eva give the name 'Mrs Birling' when she sought help from the charity?	Because, being pregnant and unmarried, she would have been discriminated against

Now turn to pages 112–113 and complete Practice questions 24–25.

Knowledge

Exam skills

You must know the text well to write a successful exam response. Make sure you are familiar with the plot, method, character, and themes before attempting this and the next section.

Choosing an examination question

In your examination, you will be presented with two questions and you must choose *one* to answer. For example:

Either

> How does Priestley explore the importance of wealth in the play?
>
> Write about:
> - what Priestley shows about attitudes to money through the characters
> - how Priestley presents the importance of money in the play.
>
> [30 marks]
> AO4 [4 marks]

or

> How far is Eric presented as a guilty character?
>
> Write about:
> - what Eric says and does
> - how Priestley uses Eric to explore ideas about guilt.
>
> [30 marks]
> AO4 [4 marks]

REMEMBER
- Choose one question. It is worth 30 marks. You have 50 minutes to answer.
- Both questions have the same number of marks, so choose the one you feel you will answer best.

EXAM TIP
The two bullet points under the main question are to help you to respond fully and to organise your answer.

Understanding your question

To make sure you understand your chosen question, you can underline and make notes on it. For example:

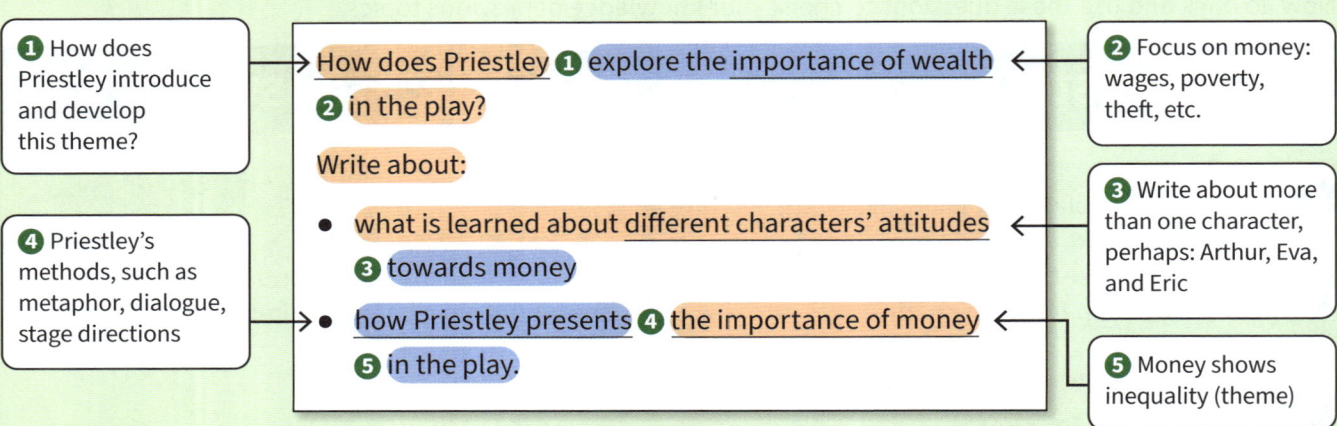

Planning

Spend a few minutes planning your response. You could make a bullet point list or a quick mind map, such as this one.

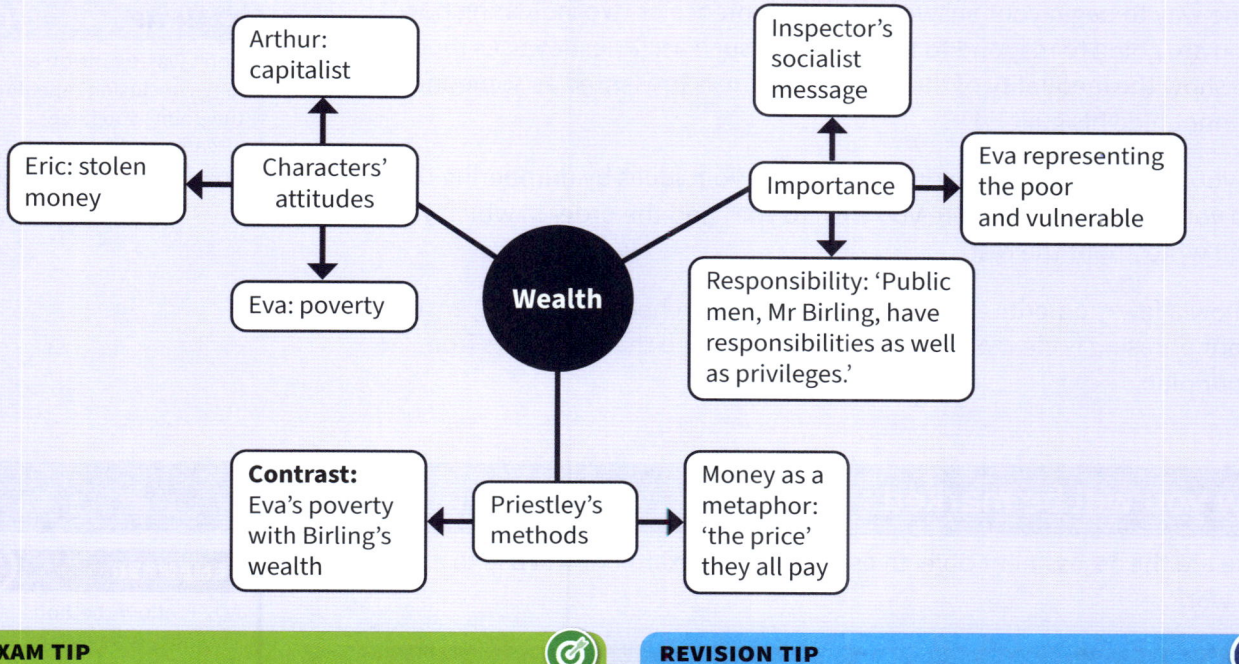

> **EXAM TIP**
> Read the question carefully. Every year there are students who confuse which characters are the focus of the question or forget to write about one of the bullet points.

> **REVISION TIP**
> Use some of the questions on pages 103–115 and practise annotating them.

Textual references

You are expected to support your ideas with references to the text. These might be:

- short quotations. For example: 'Eva is presented sympathetically by Gerald as "pretty and warm-hearted" and, after he broke off relations, "gallant"'.
- relevant details. For example: 'The play takes place over one evening, in one room, adding to its claustrophobic atmosphere'.
- brief explorations or linking of key moments. For example: 'The engagement ring is an important prop showing the changes in Sheila's relationship with Gerald, including her acceptance, her rejection, and her ultimate postponement of the engagement'.
- pinpointing important moments in the play. For example: 'The moment when the Inspector silences the Birlings before his speech signals the play's climax'.

> **REVISION TIP**
> You are not expected to memorise long quotations or to fill your answer with lots of them. If you do learn quotations, choose short, memorable ones that can be used in a variety of questions. You will not be penalised for slightly incorrect quotations.

Knowledge **95**

Knowledge

Exam skills

Organising your ideas

- One way to begin your answer is with a sentence or two indicating how you are going to respond to the question, such as: 'Priestley uses money to show the inequality of the society' or 'Eric is presented as someone who cannot hide his guilt'.

- If you have made a plan, you can organise your ideas by numbering them, so you are confident where you wish to start and the order in which you will write about the rest.

- Allow a few moments at the end of the exam to check your work, ensuring your phrasing is clear and that you have included the key points from your plan.

> **EXAM TIP**
> Don't waste time on a long conclusion repeating the points you have already made.

How you will be marked

These are the assessment objectives (or AOs) the examiner will use to assess your work.

Assessment Objective	Explanation	What this means in the *An Inspector Calls* section of the exam
AO1	How well you answer the question and understand the text	Your focus and insight into the question and the quality of your writing.
AO1	How well you choose parts of the text to support your answer	Use of textual references, such as short quotations, key moments, or details relevant to the question.
AO2	How well you explain what the writer has done to create meanings	Your understanding of how Priestley uses drama to convey his ideas, such as language and structure.
AO2	Your use of subject vocabulary linked to meanings	Correct use of literary and dramatic terminology, as appropriate.
AO3	How well you explain the ideas shown in the text	Your understanding of the world of the play and the ideas explored in it.

> **REMEMBER**
> AO2 is about methods. This means anything that Priestley does to present the story, such as what he has the characters doing and saying, the way the play begins, develops and ends, settings, dialogue, and stage directions.

> **EXAM TIP**
> When fulfilling AO3, you may make brief reference to the context in which the play is set or written if it relates to the question, but don't include irrelevant historical context. The emphasis is on the world of the play: the characters' beliefs, circumstances, and concerns as communicated by the playwright.

Meeting the assessment objectives

The examiners will assess your overall achievement, rather than give a separate mark for each AO. The level you are assigned will be the 'best fit' for your answer, even if some elements are above or below the overall level.

Level 1 1–5 marks	Level 2 6–10 marks	Level 3 11–15 marks
Simple	**Relevant**	**Explained**
• occasional focus on the question • simple points made • little engagement with ideas or methods • some misunderstandings • phrasing might be unclear	• question focus generally secure • relevant if underdeveloped ideas • generally competent understanding • phrasing mainly clear • some engagement with ideas • basic grasp of methods	• focus on the question secure • points are explained using examples and explanation • competent understanding • phrasing mainly clear • some engagement with ideas • sound grasp of methods

Level 4 16–20 marks	Level 5 21–25 marks	Level 6 26–30 marks
Clear	**Thoughtful**	**Conceptual**
• focus on the question secure • points are clear and developed • clear and secure understanding • clear phrasing • clear engagement with ideas • clear grasp of methods	• focus on the question secure • points are clear and developed with insight • clear and secure understanding with useful details • clear phrasing • clear and thoughtful engagement with ideas • clear grasp of methods	• focus on the question secure • points explore ideas at a high level • insightful understanding with useful details • clear/fluent phrasing • perceptive engagement with ideas • perceptive grasp of methods

> **EXAM TIP**
> Using textual references is a way of supporting your ideas with details and to avoid making overly general or incorrect points.

> **EXAM TIP**
> Aim to write clearly in your handwriting and your phrasing. Sometimes, trying to write in a really complex way can make your answer difficult for the examiner to understand.

Knowledge

Sample answers

Sample answer 1 – Lower level

Here is an extract from a student response to this exam-style question, with the examiner's annotations and final comments. This response receives less than half marks.

> How does Priestley present relationships between parents and children?
>
> **[30 marks]**
>
> **AO4 [4 marks]**

The Birling family are 'very pleased' with themselves. This makes it seem like they are happy. ❶ As the father of the family, Arthur expects to be listened to because he tells the others to pay attention and then delivers long speeches. This shows that he is a strong character. ❷ On the other hand, Sybil speaks less. While the family may seem to be a happy one at first, after the Inspector's arrival, it is clear that all is not well. ❸ Sheila becomes ashamed of how her parents are reacting to the Inspector, as she is more willing to be guilty and thinks they are too guilty as well. ❹ Also Sheila puts Eric in it by saying that he should take responsibility for Eva and the baby. ❺ Although Sybil spoke little in the first act, by the second act she is in conflict with Sheila and, by Act 3, Eric is furious with her. Then Arthur turns off Eric and says 'I blame you' to him. ❻

❶ Makes an appropriate textual reference, but with a basic explanation

❷ This is a competent explanation.

❸ Notes a turning point

❹ The phrasing is a little confusing here.

❺ This is a mistake - it is Sybil, not Sheila who says the father of Eva's baby should take responsibility.

❻ Conflict is identified and the textual reference is correct, but this could be explained more clearly

Examiner's comments

This response shows an understanding of the relationships in the play and includes textual references with explanations. Methods are only lightly touched upon, such as the idea of 'conflict' and structure. More insight into, and engagement with, Priestley's ideas is needed.

Sample answer 2 – Mid level

Here is an extract from a student response to the exam-style question on page 98, with the examiner's annotations and final comments. This response receives around half marks.

① Starts with a clear focus and grasps the importance of the setting

③ Appropriate textual reference

⑤ Clear account of conflict

⑥ These important points are rushed and need more textual support.

> Priestley presents the relationship between parents and children as extremely important. The play is set in the family home during the celebration of Sheila's engagement. **①** Arthur takes the lead as the man of the house. His business success has given him confidence in his ability to support his family. The rest of the family goes along with what he wants. He lectures them at length and they, mainly, seem to listen to him. **②** Sybil is described as 'rather cold' and she doesn't seem to understand her children, particularly Eric, who is a heavy drinker, but she thinks he is just 'a boy'. **③** In Act 2, she thinks she is defending her family by trying to get the Inspector to leave, but she actually makes things worse. **④** The biggest conflicts are in Act 3. In particular, Eric is furious at what he thinks is Sybil's betrayal of him, which causes Eva and the baby's death. As Sybil thought of him as a boy, it is clear that she is entirely shocked by Eric's anger which is 'almost threatening'. **⑤** Arthur seems to respect Gerald more than Eric. Priestley presents Eric as a huge contrast to Arthur and also a disappointment to him. **⑥** Priestley is showing that the generations do not always get along and that the younger generation will listen more to the Inspector about society. **⑦**

② Demonstrates a good understanding of the character of Arthur

④ Clear understanding but more detail and insight needed

⑦ This needs more analysis and connection to Priestley's larger themes, such as social responsibility.

Examiner's comments

This is a clear response which maintains focus on the members of the family, though more insight is needed into the relationships.

REVISION TIP

Practise timed writings so that you don't rush the final paragraphs of your answer.

Knowledge 99

Knowledge

Sample answers

Sample answer 3 – Higher level

Here is an extract from a student response to the exam-style question on page 98, with the examiner's annotations and final comments. This response receives high marks.

> Priestley presents the relationships between the parents and children in the Birling family as important, yet flawed and uses the Birling family to criticise inequality and prejudices. The Inspector's revelations show the cracks that lie beneath the surface of society, as well as of this successful family. ❶ The Birlings can provide financial security to their children, in contrast to the precarious life of an orphan like Eva. The opening stage directions emphasise the united appearance of the family, comfortably gathered after a luxurious meal. However, Priestley uses foreshadowing to suggest that the relationship is not as close as it seems, with Eric's 'guffaws' and other disruptive behaviour. ❷ Priestley highlights Eric's lack of self-discipline with indications of heavy drinking and his tendency to become 'squiffy', but Eric has never had to struggle (as Eva has), as he has been supported by his family educationally and financially. ❸ The bonds between the children and their parents disintegrate after the Inspector's revelations showing that these relationships were already flawed. Eric lashes out in a manner that is 'almost threatening' at his mother, who Priestley portrays as 'cold', and admits he never confided in his father because he wasn't 'the kind of father a chap could go to when he's in trouble.' ❹

❶ A conceptual response dealing with important ideas.

❷ Considers how methods such as stage directions and foreshadowing provide insight into the family's relationships and provides textual references

❸ Offers insight into how Eric's family has benefited him, contrasting with Eva who doesn't have a family, highlighting the theme of social inequality

❹ Well-chosen textual references from stage directions and dialogue to provide insight into relationships.

5 Offers insight into relationships, based on a clear understanding of the play

This presents a stark contrast to the seemingly happy family at the start and reinforces the idea that Eric has been a disappointment to Arthur. Though his family have supported him financially, Eric is shown to have felt emotionally unsupported. **5** Sheila's engagement to Gerald provides further insight into her relationship with her parents. At first Sheila conforms to the social conventions and expectations of her parents. They are proud that her marriage will improve the family's financial and social standing. It is suggested that Sheila's marriage will reflect her parents, where the husband has 'important work to do' and the wife follows his lead. **6** After the Inspector's revelations, Sheila's attitude contrasts with that of her parents and their relationship is fractured. Priestley's stage directions show her 'quietly crying' as she processes her feelings of guilt, while her parents refuse to accept any responsibility. **7** Her strength of character is shown by her refusal to forget everything when it seems it may be all a hoax. Unlike her parents, she doesn't return to her previous unthinking happiness. Priestley uses the Birling family to show the changes necessary for a fairer society - ideas which Sheila and Eric are more willing to accept than their parents. He shows how we are all metaphorically 'members of one body', and that recognising this could lead to a fairer future. **8**

6 Nuanced analysis of Sheila's relationship with her parents

7 Clear discussion of why Sheila's relationship with her parents has changed and how the stage directions help to convey this

8 Explores the concept of the Birling family representing society and connects clearly to Priestley's wider themes

Examiner's comments

This is a confident, conceptual approach showing an ease with the ideas of the play and the writer's methods. There is perceptive analysis and it is fluently written.

LINK

To revise the topic of generations, look back at Themes on pages 89–92.

Knowledge

Retrieval

Answer the questions below. Cover the answers column with a piece of paper and write down as many answers as you can. Check and repeat.

Questions / Answers

#	Questions	Answers
1	How many questions will you have to choose from?	2
2	How many marks is your answer worth?	30
3	How long do you have to answer this question?	50 minutes
4	How many questions do you need to answer?	1
5	AO2 required you to show your understanding of Priestley's use of drama to do what?	Convey ideas and meaning
6	What type of context is required for AO3?	The world of the play – the characters' beliefs, circumstances and concerns as presented by the writer
7	Do textual references have to be quotations?	No
8	Should your conclusion repeat all the main points you've already made?	No
9	Is it necessary to learn lots of long quotations to use in the exam?	No – If you do learn quotations, choose short, memorable ones that can be used in a variety of questions.
10	Do you need to include external historical context?	No

Previous questions

Now go back and use these questions to check your knowledge of previous topics.

#	Questions	Answers
1	Give two examples of the inequality in Gerald and Daisy's relationship.	She becomes financially dependent upon him; she has greater feelings for him
2	What method is used when Arthur wrongly predicts future peace?	Irony

Practice

Exam-style questions

Use the questions in this section to practise the knowledge and skills you have learned.

1

How far does Priestley present Arthur Birling as a selfish character?

Write about:

- what Arthur says and does
- how far Priestley presents Arthur's character as admirable.

[30 marks]
AO4 [4 marks]

EXAM TIP

If a bullet point mentions what a character 'says and does' or similar words, it is not asking you just to report these. You should select the best examples of dialogue and actions to answer the question.

2

How far does Priestley present Gerald as a deceitful character in the play?

Write about:

- Gerald's words and actions
- how Priestley presents Gerald in the play.

[30 marks]
AO4 [4 marks]

3

How do Sheila's attitudes to society change in the play?

Write about:

- what Sheila says and does
- how Priestley presents Sheila to the audience.

[30 marks]
AO4 [4 marks]

EXAM TIP

If a question asks how a character changes, attempt to find evidence from several places in the play to show this, rather than focusing on just one scene.

Practice

Exam-style questions

4

How far is Sheila presented as a sympathetic character?

Write about:
- Sheila's words and actions
- how far Priestley presents her as sympathetic.

[30 marks]
AO4 [4 marks]

5

How does Priestley present the Inspector as powerful and mysterious in the play?

Write about:
- what the Inspector says and does
- how far Priestley presents him as powerful and/or mysterious.

[30 marks]
AO4 [4 marks]

6

How does Priestley use the Inspector to challenge the Birlings' beliefs?

Write about:
- the characters' reactions to what the Inspector says and does
- how Priestley presents the Inspector.

[30 marks]
AO4 [4 marks]

> **EXAM TIP**
>
> If the question directs you to write about more than one character, plan in advance which characters you are choosing and keep track of your time, so you can cover two or more characters in appropriate detail.

7

How far does Priestley present Eric as a weak character?

Write about:
- what Eric says and does
- how far Priestley presents Eric as weak.

[30 marks]
AO4 [4 marks]

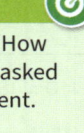

EXAM TIP

If a question asks 'How far', you are being asked to make a judgement. For example, you might argue that a character is portrayed as entirely sympathetic or unsympathetic or somewhere between the two.

8

How far is Eric presented as a guilty character in the play?

Write about:
- what Eric says and does
- how Priestley uses Eric to explore ideas about guilt.

[30 marks]
AO4 [4 marks]

9

How far is Sybil Birling presented as an unsympathetic character?

Write about:
- what Sybil says and does
- how Priestley presents her as sympathetic.

[30 marks]
AO4 [4 marks]

Practice

Exam-style questions

10

How is the character of Sybil used to explore ideas about social class?

Write about:

- what Sybil says and does
- how Priestley presents Sybil in relation to social class.

[30 marks]
AO4 [4 marks]

11

How does Priestley use the relationship between Eric and Arthur to show the generational divide?

Write about:

- what Eric and Arthur say and do
- how Priestley presents their relationship.

[30 marks]
AO4 [4 marks]

> **EXAM TIP**
>
> The 'how' in a question is usually a reminder to think about Priestley's methods such as his language choices, the play's structure, dialogue and his use of stage directions.

12

How does Priestley show the changes in the relationship between Gerald and Sheila throughout the play?

Write about:

- what Gerald and Sheila say and do
- how Priestley presents their changing relationship.

[30 marks]
AO4 [4 marks]

13

How does Priestley present the relationship between Arthur and Sybil?

Write about:
- what the characters say and do
- how Priestley presents their different relationships.

[30 marks]
AO4 [4 marks]

14

How does Priestley present Sybil's relationship with her children?

Write about:
- what their interactions are like
- how Priestley presents Sybil as a mother.

[30 marks]
AO4 [4 marks]

# Practice

Exam-style questions

15

How does Priestley present the conflict between Arthur and the Inspector?

Write about:
- what their interactions are like
- how Priestley presents when their characters are in conflict.

[30 marks]
AO4 [4 marks]

EXAM TIP
Remember that conflict can be subtle and revealed in a text through subtext and stage directions.

16

How far does Priestley present the Birlings as a happy family?

Write about:
- what their interactions are like
- how far Priestley presents them as happy.

[30 marks]
AO4 [4 marks]

17

How does Priestley present the importance of money?

Write about:

- what the characters say about money and how it affects them
- how Priestley presents its importance in the play.

[30 marks]
AO4 [4 marks]

18

How are women viewed in the society presented in the play?

Write about:

- what is said about the female characters and how they are treated
- how Priestley presents women in this society.

[30 marks]
AO4 [4 marks]

> **EXAM TIP**
> Engagement with the ideas of the play, such as what Priestley is saying about society, is important to achieve high marks.

Practice

Exam-style questions

19

How are relationships between men and women shown in the play?

Write about:

- what examples there are of these relationships
- how Priestley presents relationships between men and women.

[30 marks]
AO4 [4 marks]

EXAM TIP

Remember you can also quote from the stage directions.

20

How is the theme of inequality explored through the character of Eva Smith?

Write about:

- what inequality is experienced by Eva Smith
- how Priestley presents Eva Smith and inequality.

[30 marks]
AO4 [4 marks]

EXAM TIP

If a question asks you to write about how a character is used to explore an idea or theme, remember to keep the focus on the named character, even if you have a lot you would like to say about other characters.

21

How does Priestley present the importance of social class in the play?

Write about:

- what examples there are of different social classes
- how Priestley presents the effects of social class.

[30 marks]
AO4 [4 marks]

22

How does Priestley show different attitudes to responsibility?

Write about:

- what dialogue and actions show about the characters' attitudes to responsibility
- how Priestley presents these attitudes and their importance in the play.

[30 marks]
AO4 [4 marks]

> **EXAM TIP**
> Using some of the wording of the question in your answer will help to keep you correctly focused.

Practice

Exam-style questions

23

How does Priestley present reactions to guilt?

Write about:
- what can be learned of different characters' reactions to guilt
- how Priestley presents guilt in the play.

[30 marks]
AO4 [4 marks]

24

How does Priestley explore ideas about older and younger generations in the play?

Write about:
- what characters from each generation say and do
- how Priestley presents the different generations.

[30 marks]
AO4 [4 marks]

25

'The younger generation are the hope for the future.'

How far do you agree with this view in *An Inspector Calls*?

Write about:
- what the younger characters say and do
- how Priestley presents them as providing hope or not.

[30 marks]
AO4 [4 marks]

EXAM TIP

Statement questions provide a springboard for discussing important ideas. You do not have to entirely agree with the statement, but you should use it to explore your thoughts.

26

'Beneath many apparently happy families lie deceptions and disappointments.'

How far do you agree that this view applies to the Birlings in *An Inspector Calls*?

Write about:
- what the Birlings do and say
- how Priestley presents the Birlings as a family.

[30 marks]
AO4 [4 marks]

Practice

Exam-style questions

27

'Despite both being young women, Eva and Sheila are presented as opposites.'

How far do you agree with this view of *An Inspector Calls*?

Write about:

- the characters of Eva and Sheila
- how Priestley compares and contrasts their characters.

[30 marks]
AO4 [4 marks]

28

'Arthur and the Inspector represent opposite points of view on society.'

How far do you agree with this view of *An Inspector Calls*?

Write about:

- what points of view Arthur and the Inspector express
- how Priestley presents their points of view and to what extent they are opposites.

[30 marks]
AO4 [4 marks]

EXAM TIP

Be careful of overusing the simple point–quotation–explanation structure as that can make your writing less fluent and engaging.

29

'The Birlings are responsible for Eva Smith's death'.

How far do you agree with this statement?

Write about:
- the role of the Birlings
- other factors contributing to Eva's problems.

[30 marks]
AO4 [4 marks]

EXAM TIP
Remember you are writing about a play so use the appropriate terminology such as acts, dialogue and stage directions.

30

'We are all responsible for each other.'

How does Priestley explore this idea in the play?

Write about:
- the characters' different attitudes towards responsibility
- how Priestley presents responsibility.

[30 marks]
AO4 [4 marks]

Great Clarendon Street, Oxford, OX2 6DP, United Kingdom

Oxford University Press is a department of the University of Oxford. It furthers the University's objective of excellence in research, scholarship, and education by publishing worldwide. Oxford is a registered trade mark of Oxford University Press in the UK and in certain other countries.

© Oxford University Press 2025

Series Editor: Lyndsay Bawden

Written by Annie Fox

The moral rights of the authors have been asserted

First published in 2025

All rights reserved. No part of this publication may be reproduced, stored in a retrieval system, transmitted, used for text and data mining, or used for training artificial intelligence, in any form or by any means, without the prior permission in writing of Oxford University Press, or as expressly permitted by law, by licence or under terms agreed with the appropriate reprographics rights organization. Enquiries concerning reproduction outside the scope of the above should be sent to the Rights Department, Oxford University Press, at the address above.

You must not circulate this work in any other form and you must impose this same condition on any acquirer

British Library Cataloguing in Publication Data

Data available

978-1-382-06748-5

978-1-382-06747-8 (ebook)

10 9 8 7 6 5 4 3 2 1

The manufacturing process conforms to the environmental regulations of the country of origin.

Printed in the UK by Bell & Bain.

The manufacturer's authorised representative in the EU for product safety is Oxford University Press España S.A. of El Parque Empresarial San Fernando de Henares, Avenida de Castilla, 2 - 28830 Madrid (www.oup.es/en or productsafety@oup.com). OUP España S.A. also acts an importer into Spain of products made by the manufacturer.

Acknowledgements

The publisher would like to thank Jade Hickin and Sarah Cottinghatt for sharing their expertise and feedback in the development of this resource.

The publisher would like to thank the following for permissions to use copyright material:

An Inspector Calls, copyright © J.B. Priestley 1947, from J.B. Priestley: *An Inspector Calls and Other Plays* (Penguin, 1969, 2000). Reprinted by permission of United Agents on behalf of The Estate of the late J.B. Priestley

Although we have made every effort to trace and contact all copyright holders before publication, this has not been possible in all cases. If notified, the publisher will rectify any errors or omissions at the earliest opportunity.